THE
DECORATED PORCH

CREATIVE PROJECTS FROM LESLIE BECK

LESLIE BECK
OF FIBER MOSAICS

Martingale
& COMPANY™

CREDITS

President ∾ Nancy J. Martin
CEO/Publisher ∾ Daniel J. Martin
Associate Publisher ∾ Jane Hamada
Editorial Director ∾ Mary V. Green
Editorial Project Manager ∾ Tina Cook
Technical Editor ∾ Laurie Baker
Copy Editor ∾ Ellen Balstad
Design and Production Manager ∾ Stan Green
Illustrators ∾ Pat Wagner and Michael Rohani
Cover and Text Designer ∾ Rohani Design
Photographer ∾ Brent Kane

The Decorated Porch: Creative Projects from Leslie Beck
© 2001 by Leslie Beck

Martingale & Company
20205 144th Avenue NE
Woodinville, WA 98072-8478 USA
www.martingale-pub.com

Printed in China
06 05 04 03 02 01   8 7 6 5 4 3 2 1

Library of Congress Cataloging-in-Publication Data

Beck, Leslie.
   The decorated porch : creative projects from Leslie Beck / Leslie Beck.
      p. cm.
   ISBN 1-56477-362-0
   1. Handicraft. 2. Porches–Decoration–United States. 3. Textile fabrics in interior decoration. I. Title.

TT157 .B359 2001
747.7'9–dc21   2001022256

ACKNOWLEDGMENTS

This book was developed with the help and dedication of my talented team:

Retta Warehime, quilt designer and author, who led my staff through many hours of measuring, cutting, sewing, writing, and editing.

Debbie Baalman, Shirley Christensen, Jerrine Kirsch, Gayla Winsor, Shawna Holland, and Lera Beck, who sewed and proofed the projects. Thanks for your excellence.

Kathy Renzelman and Teresa Houlihan for their skill in the art of decorative painting.

Special recognition goes to Patty Wagner for drawing the illustrations, Earlene Sullivan and Judith Leebolt-Bourne for editing the manuscript, and Chris Cordle, Kate Beck, and Byron Beck for generating the computer graphics.

Thanks to all for the team effort and commitment.

DEDICATION

To my husband, Byron Sr., and my children, Byron Jr., Christine, and Kate. Their belief and support urge me forward; their love and patience help me pursue my design career.

And to Martingale & Company for their encouragement, direction, and expertise in bringing this book to life.

CONTENTS

INTRODUCTION

❧━◆━◇━◆━❧

Enjoying the outdoors has returned to the American scene as a popular pastime for many people. Because we all work hard at whatever we do, we need to take time out to relax, too. Leaving work behind, putting your feet up, and enjoying the sights and sounds of the outdoors from your own cozy porch is one way to experience this relaxation. With this book, I hope to tempt you to decorate your porch so it provides an inviting atmosphere all year long. To do that, I've created collections of projects based on each of the four seasons. You will find quilts, pillows, tablecloths, painted accessories, and much more to entice you to leave work behind and find time for yourself.

For those of you who aren't blessed with a porch, many of these projects are equally suitable for a sunroom, four-season room, or even a family room. Create an environment that keeps you in tune with the serenity and beauty of nature, and enjoy your return to the great outdoors.

GENERAL SEWING INSTRUCTIONS

Supplies

The following tools and supplies will make it easier for you to create the sewn projects in this book. For those who've already experienced the relaxation that comes with sewing, these items are basic. All you'll need to add is fabric—and selecting new pieces is always fun!

Iron and Ironing Board

An iron and ironing board are essential as you'll want to press frequently and carefully to ensure smooth, accurately stitched results. An experienced quilter may tell you that she spends more time pressing than sewing. Add a Teflon pressing sheet for fusing together appliqué pieces.

Needles

Use sewing-machine needles sized for cotton fabrics, such as 70/10 or 80/12. Keep a sharp needle in the machine. A dull needle interferes with tension and causes skipped, loose, or uneven stitches. In addition, keep an assortment of hand sewing and quilting needles available in sizes such as #8, #9, and #10.

> *Tip* A popping sound as the needle pierces the fabric is a good clue that it is time to change your sewing machine needle.

Pins

Keep a good supply of glass- or plastic-headed pins nearby. Long pins are especially helpful for pinning multiple layers together. A visit to your local quilt shop will help you decide which pins are best for your project.

Rotary Cutter and Mat

A large rotary cutter enables you to quickly cut the strips and pieces you'll need for most of these projects. A self-healing mat protects both the cutter blade and tabletop.

Rotary-Cutting Rulers

You'll need a rotary-cutting ruler to measure fabric and to guide the rotary cutter. There are many appropriate rulers, but one of my favorites is the 24" acrylic type that includes gridded lines for cutting strips, guidelines for marking and cutting 45° and 60° angles, and ¼" increments marked along the edge. A guide such as a Bias Square® is useful for squaring up blocks and for making certain that the long ruler is properly positioned on the fabric for rotary cutting (see page 7). Visit your local quilt shop to choose your own personal favorites from the many options available.

Sewing Machine

You don't need anything fancy: just a reliable straight-stitch machine in good working order. Adjust the stitch length so the stitches hold seams in place securely, but are easy to remove if necessary. Of key importance is the ability to gauge an accurate ¼" seam allowance. If you do not have a ¼" foot for your machine, contact your machine dealer or local quilt shop for assistance, or mark your machine as suggested in "Machine Piecing" on page 9.

Thread

Use a good-quality, all-purpose thread that is either 100 percent cotton, cotton-wrapped polyester, or polyester. Do not use prewaxed hand quilting thread in your sewing machine.

Fabric

While it is not necessary to purchase the most expensive fabric, a good rule of thumb in selecting fabric is to buy the best you can afford. Light- to medium-weight 100 percent–cotton fabric produces the best results in any quilting project. Good-quality cotton is reasonably uniform, wrinkle-free, and closely woven with long, fine threads. Avoid poor-quality fabric that wrinkles easily and is uneven or loosely woven with short, weak threads.

Color is a personal choice. The only person to please is you. If you are unsure how to select colors that will look nice together in a finished project, try the "blender technique." A blender fabric is one with four or more colors. Choose a fabric print you really love and use this print as a palette to select additional fabrics. The fabric designer has already done the work of

coordinating the colors for you! If you like the colors in the blender fabric and choose those colors for coordinating fabrics, chances are you will be pleased with the finished project.

Arrange your fabric choices on the background fabric you've chosen, and then stand back. Take off your glasses, squint, or use a Ruby Beholder® value-finding tool to see if any fabrics blend too closely. For best results, include a good range of lights, mediums, and darks, and keep each value distinct. If any of the fabrics are too close in value, substitute another fabric until you have the right contrast.

View the scale of the prints in relation to how they will be used in the project. If you need just a small piece in the block, use a small-scale print. A large-scale print is better showcased in a larger piece.

The fabric amounts listed for the individual projects assume that the fabric is at least 42" wide after laundering and pressing.

Techniques

The following are some basic cutting, stitching, and embellishing guidelines to help you complete the projects in this book.

Rotary Cutting

The pieced projects in *The Decorated Porch* do not require templates. You'll rotary cut strips, crosscut strips into smaller segments, and combine them to complete the necessary blocks and units. All rotary measurements include ¼"-wide seam allowances, unless otherwise noted.

Note: Reverse the following rotary-cutting techniques if you are left-handed.

1. Fold the fabric in half lengthwise, matching the selvages. Place the fabric on the cutting mat so that the length of fabric lies to your right, with the raw edges on the left.

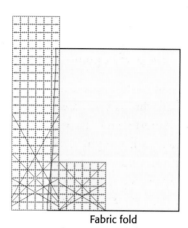

Fabric fold

2. Align a Bias Square ruler with the fold and place a long ruler against it. Remove the Bias Square and press firmly on the long ruler to keep it from moving. Place the cutter blade next to the ruler and, exerting an even pressure on the rotary cutter, begin cutting. Always roll the cutter away from yourself! As you cut, move your fingers along the ruler as necessary to hold it steadily in place. After cutting, check to see if all the layers have been cut. If not, try again, this time applying more pressure to the cutter.

3. Keeping the fabric to your right, use the ruler to measure a strip of the appropriate width from the left straight edge. If, for instance, you need a 2½" x 42" strip of fabric, align the fabric edge with the 2½" line on the ruler and cut along the ruler's edge.

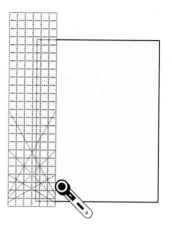

4. Turn the strip horizontally and cut to the desired shape and size.

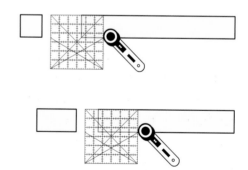

Machine Piecing

Accuracy is important when machine piecing. Unless otherwise noted, place the pieces right sides together and use a ¼"-wide seam allowance to stitch the pieces together. Move the needle position so that it is ¼" from the right side of the presser foot, or measure ¼" to the right of the needle and mark the seam allowance on the sewing machine with a piece of masking tape. For many of today's machines, you also can buy a presser foot that measures ¼" from the needle to the presser foot outside edge.

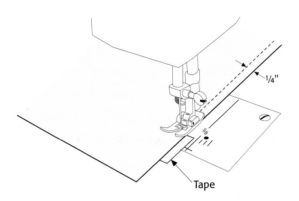

Tape

Often you can save time and thread by chain-piecing. Place pieces to be joined right sides together and pin as necessary. Stitch the seam, but do not lift the presser foot or cut the connecting threads; just feed in the next pair of pieces. Join as many pairs as possible; then clip the threads between the pieces.

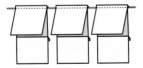

MATCHING SEAMS AND POINTS

It is not always easy to line up seams and match points perfectly, especially if you rely on chance! Try these simple techniques to help achieve perfect points.

• Poke a pin into one point along the seam line and through to the seam or other point it must match. Slide the fabric pieces together until the pin is perpendicular to the fabric and the pieces line up. Pin securely on both sides of the point you are matching. Remove the first pin and stitch.

• Whenever possible, work with opposing seam allowances. When matching seam lines for sewing, make sure the seam allowance on the bottom layer is pressed so that it moves easily over the feed dogs; then press the top seam allowance in the opposite direction. This "locks" the seams into position so you can line them up exactly. Pin the seam allowances in place if necessary.

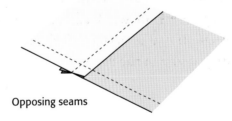

Opposing seams

• If the pieces being joined are slightly different in length, pin the pieces together at the ends and at the seam; then sew with the longer piece on the bottom, against the feed dogs. The feed dogs will ease the fullness on the bottom piece, coaxing both pieces past the needle together.

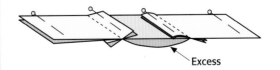

Excess

Tip For extra-tricky junctions, stitch 1" to ¾" from the intersection and stop with the needle down. Set the sewing machine for a longer stitch length; then continue stitching ¾" to 1" past the intersection. With the needle down, return to the standard stitch length and resume stitching. When you finish the seam, check to see if the points match. If they do, simply restitch over the long stitches. If not, you can easily remove the long stitches, adjust, re-pin, and try again until the points match.

Pressing

Place a freshly laundered, folded towel on the ironing board when pressing blocks. The towel helps ease out any unwanted fullness, so the project will lie flat.

Use a dry iron set on the cotton setting and a spray bottle filled with water to create steam. Using the steam feature on your iron can distort pieces (especially smaller ones) and even alter the block shape because of the temperature and force at which the steam is emitted from the iron. Always test the iron temperature on a scrap of fabric before pressing the project piece to avoid scorching the fabric.

Develop the habit of pressing each seam as it is sewn. Turn the piece to the wrong side and "tack press" by lightly touching the iron to the seam allowance to get it started in the right direction. On the right side, spray lightly with water and press with gentle pressure from the center out. Check the block wrong side to make sure all seams are pressed correctly before proceeding.

Appliqué

Some of the projects in this book include appliquéd motifs. Full-size patterns are provided for these projects. *These patterns do not include seam allowances.* Refer to the project instructions for positioning the appliqués on the project.

Two methods of appliqué follow. *Note that all appliqué templates are printed in reverse of how the motif appears in the finished project to make them suitable for the fusible-web technique. Be sure to flip over the templates if you plan to appliqué by hand or are using the templates in a painted project.*

Fusible-Web Appliqué

Fusible-web appliqué is a quick, efficient alternative to the hand-appliqué method and gives the finished project a wonderful folk-art look. Each shape is traced directly onto a paper-backed fusible bonding agent, which is applied with an iron to the wrong side of the appliqué fabric. The shape is cut and the paper removed. Then the fabric shape is heat-bonded to the background block and finished with a decorative hand or machine stitch.

There are many fusible products on the market. Experiment to find the one that best suits your needs, and be sure to read and follow the manufacturer's instructions.

Remember: Because the fusible material is bonded to the wrong side of the fabric, the appliqué patterns for the projects in this book have been printed in reverse. When the shape is flipped over to be bonded to the background, the appliqué appears correctly on the finished project.

Tip If the base fabric will be seen through the appliqué fabric, apply fusible woven interfacing to the wrong side of the fabric before fusing the bonding agent to the appliqué piece. Be sure to pre-wash and air-dry the interfacing before applying it to the fabric.

1. Trace the appropriate appliqué patterns directly onto fusible material; cut out around the traced designs, leaving a ⅛" margin.
2. Fuse the traced designs to the wrong side of the appropriate appliqué fabric, cut on the drawn lines, and remove the paper backing.
3. When the appliqué involves more than one piece, fuse the pieces together before adhering them to the background. Use a Teflon pressing sheet under and over the appliqué pieces to protect the fabric, the iron, and the ironing surface from the fusible product.
4. Refer to the instructions and finished project photo for guidance in positioning the appliqués in place.
5. Machine stitch the fused design to the background using a blanket stitch or a very short (⅛"-wide) zigzag stitch.

Note: *If tear-away stabilizer is required for a project, cut the stabilizer 1" or 2" larger than the appliqué and place the stabilizer between the project and the feed dogs. Typing or other lightweight paper may be used as a substitute stabilizer.*

Hand Appliqué

Hand appliqué involves applying (or stitching) a motif to a background block or unit. It is done with an invisible stitch, using matching thread and a small (size #11 or #12), fine appliqué needle.

1. Transfer the appropriate pattern pieces to cardboard or template plastic. *Remember:* Because the patterns are reversed for the fusible method, you will need to turn them over for hand appliqué unless they are symmetrical.
2. Place the template on the right side of the fabric, reversing if necessary, and trace with a sharp pencil. Cut out the shape, adding a ¼"-wide seam allowance. After cutting, clip into the seam allowance on inside curves only.
3. Turn the fabric raw edge to the wrong side on the drawn line and baste with a light-colored thread.

Tip When basting points, such as the tip of a leaf or the bottom of a heart, fold the point back first; then fold over each side.

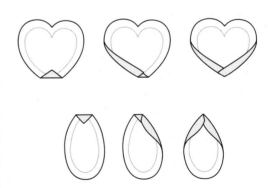

4. Pin the basted motifs in place, referring to the instructions or finished project photo to position the pieces.

5. Appliqué the pieces. Use thread that matches the color of the appliqué.

- Knot the thread and bring the needle up from the wrong side, through the background fabric, barely catching the folded edge of the appliqué.

- Insert the needle into the background fabric beside the folded edge, as close as possible to the place where the thread came through the background fabric. Travel under the background fabric to make a tiny 1/8" stitch; then bring the needle once again through the background fabric and the appliqué's folded edge. Continue around the perimeter of the shape, making snug, even stitches. Use the point of the needle to turn and smooth the fabric on curved edges.

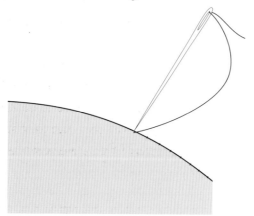

Bring the needle straight back down.

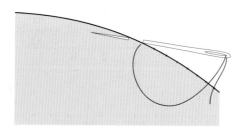

6. Finish with a knot on the wrong side of the appliquéd piece; remove the basting stitches.

Finishing

The following instructions will help you assemble finished blocks to make a quilt or wall hanging. Some of the techniques described—for example, easy-turn finishing—will also be used to complete various accessories.

Adding Borders

Finished measurements of quilts and wall hangings may vary slightly due to personal cutting and sewing techniques. While specific border measurements are listed for the projects, I recommend that you double-check and adjust border measurements as necessary before sewing borders to your quilt. Carefully matching measurements helps to keep quilts square and avoid rippled borders.

Note: The borders for all projects in this book are straight rather than mitered.

1. Measure the quilt top through its vertical center. Cut side strips to that length. Mark the midpoints of both the side border strips and the quilt top. Place the border strips and quilt top right sides together, pinning to match ends and midpoints. Add additional pins to ease as necessary. Stitch the border strips to the quilt top with a 1/4"-wide seam allowance and press the seams toward the border.

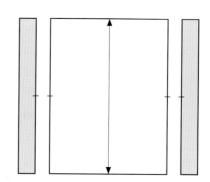

2. Measure the quilt top through its horizontal center, including the side borders. Cut the top and bottom border strips to that length. Mark the midpoints of both the border strips and the quilt top. Place the border strips and quilt top right sides together, pinning to match ends and midpoints. Add additional pins to ease as necessary. Stitch the border strips to the quilt top with a ¼"-wide seam allowance and press the seams toward the border.

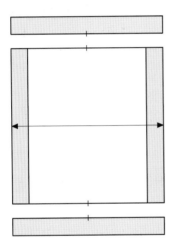

Choosing Batting and Backing

Choosing the right batting and backing for a project is just as important as the selection of fabric for the top. Consider durability, appearance, and the way the quilt will be used, cared for, and cleaned when making your decision.

Personal batting preferences vary. Take time to try different quilting techniques on different types and weights of batting to develop a feel for the look you want and the way the batting handles.

The batting choices for a wall hanging will be different than those made for a bed quilt. For wall hangings, choose a thin batting (100 percent cotton or cotton blend) that will hang flat against the wall. These ultra-thin battings can be machine or hand quilted.

For larger projects, high-loft polyester batting gives a fat, cushiony look. These thick battings are more difficult to needle, but can be machine quilted or tied. Low-loft cotton or cotton-blend batting gives a supple, traditional look, and is perfect for hand quilting.

While muslin is the traditional choice for backing, consider using a single print, or even piecing strips and scraps together until you have a backing of the desired size. Using a variety of fabrics is a great way to use leftovers and to create an interesting quilt back. Consider also whether you plan to machine or hand quilt your work. If you intend to hand quilt, choose a solid or almost solid backing fabric to showcase your beautiful hand stitches, as well as one that allows a quilting needle to glide through comfortably. Do not use bed sheets for your backing since most sheets are difficult to push a needle through.

Cut the backing 4" larger than the size of the finished top. For large quilts, there are 90"- and 108"-wide fabrics available. If it is necessary to piece the backing to get the necessary size, join two or three lengths of fabric as shown and press the seams open.

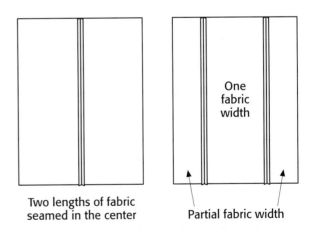

Two lengths of fabric seamed in the center

One fabric width

Partial fabric width

Assembling the Layers

"Sandwiching" is the term commonly used to describe joining the three quilt layers. Begin by laying the backing, wrong side up, on a flat surface, such as a tabletop or floor. Secure it with masking tape around all four edges. Take care to smooth out all the wrinkles, but don't distort it by pulling too tightly.

Next, smooth the batting on top of the backing. Make sure it covers the entire backing. Complete the "sandwich" by laying the quilt top, right side up, on the batting and smoothing out any wrinkles from the center to the outside edges.

> *Tip* If the batting is very wrinkled, spray it lightly with water and throw it into a dryer set on low for approximately five minutes.

For smaller projects (or those you plan to quilt by machine), pin-baste with 1"-long rust-proof safety pins. Space the pins 4" to 6" apart, working from the center out and avoiding any marked quilting lines.

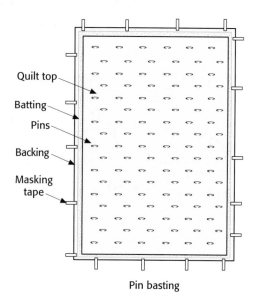

Pin basting

For larger projects (or those you plan to hand quilt), hand baste the layers together. Use a long needle and light-colored thread to take large stitches from the center to the quilt's outer top edge. Return to the center, basting to the quilt's outer bottom edge; then baste to the right and left edges. Continue basting from the center out, creating a star-burst pattern.

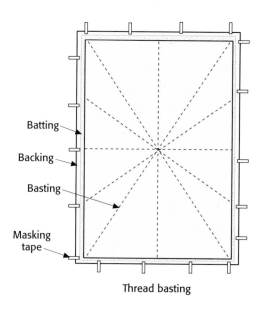

Thread basting

Securing the Layers

Quilting

For many of the projects in this book, you will be advised to machine or hand quilt your project "as desired." In the past, most quilts were quilted by hand. Today, quiltmakers have the advantage of choosing either method or a combination of both. Time and the intended use of the quilt are the usual deciding factors.

There are many excellent books to guide you, whether you choose to hand or machine quilt. *Loving Stitches* by Jeana Kimball offers expert instructions on hand quilting. For machine quilting, refer to *Machine Quilting Made Easy* by Maurine Noble. Both are published by That Patchwork Place/Martingale & Co. and are available through your local quilt shop or favorite mail-order source.

When the quilting is complete, remove the pins or long basting stitches and trim the batting and backing to the size of the quilt top.

Tying

Other projects throughout this book will instruct you to tie layers together with yarn or thread. Embroidery floss, pearl cotton, and worsted-weight yarns are the most common choices. When selecting yarn, choose one that is thin enough to pull through the fabric without damaging it. You will also need a darning or tapestry needle with an eye large enough to accommodate the yarn or threads.

Follow the instructions below to make knots that tie on the quilt front.

1. Thread the needle with 1 long length of yarn, 4 strands of pearl cotton, or 6 strands of embroidery floss. Leave the end unknotted.
2. Beginning and ending on the quilt top, take a small stitch through all layers at the position indicated in the project instructions; leave a 3" to 4" tail. Leaving a long length of yarn, continue to the next tie position and take another stitch. The length of yarn between stitches will be cut and used to tie the knot, so be sure to leave a generous amount. Any excess can be trimmed away later. Continue making stitches at each tie position, rethreading the needle as necessary.

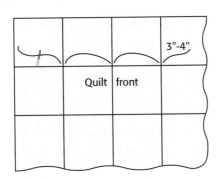

3. Cut the yarn between each tie position and tie the right tail of yarn over the left tail of

yarn; then wrap the left tail of yarn over the right tail of yarn to complete the knot. For a fuller tie, lay several 6" lengths of yarn or thread over the tie point before tying the knot.

Finishing the Edges

French Binding

Most of the quilts and wall hangings in this book are finished using French binding. This binding, constructed from a double thickness of fabric, is attractive, sturdy, and wears well.

For straight-cut French binding, use a ruler and rotary cutter to cut binding strips 2½" x 42". Be sure to cut perfectly straight across the folded width of the fabric.

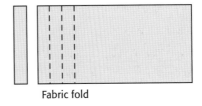

Fabric fold

Straight-cut binding

For bias-cut French binding, open up the fabric and lay it flat. Align the 45° line on your rotary cutting ruler with one of the selvage edges of the fabric. Cut along the ruler edge and trim off the corner. Cut the bias strips the desired width, measuring from the edge of the initial bias cut.

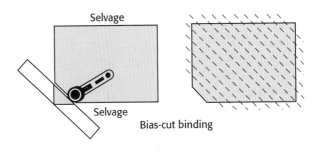

Bias-cut binding

To join straight-cut or bias-cut strips, follow these steps:

1. Place 2 strips right sides together, crossing the ends at right angles as shown. Lay them on a flat surface and pin.

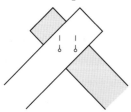

2. Imagine the strips as a large letter A and draw a line across the strips where they intersect to form the crossbar as shown. Sew directly on the line.

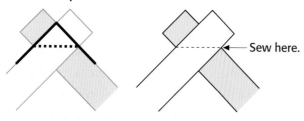

Sew here.

3. Trim the excess fabric, leaving a ¼"-wide seam allowance.

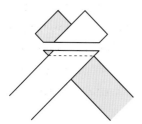

4. Press the seam open.

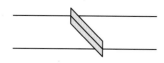

5. Fold the binding strips in half lengthwise, wrong sides together, and press.

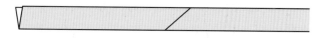

6. To determine the length of the top and bottom bindings, measure the width of the quilt through its horizontal center and cut 2 strips to that measurement. Match the top and bottom raw edges of the quilt with the raw edges of the binding, right sides together. Pin, then sew the binding to the quilt with a ¼"-wide seam allowance. Fold the binding over the seam allowance to the back of the quilt and hand stitch in place along the seam line.

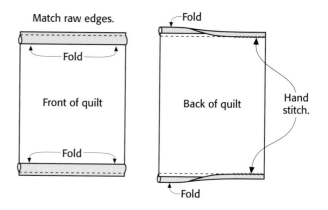

Match raw edges.

Fold

Front of quilt

Fold

Fold

Back of quilt

Hand stitch.

Fold

7. For the side bindings, measure the length of the quilt through its vertical center, add 1" to this measurement, and cut 2 binding strips to that length. For a clean-finished edge, fold each end under ½" and press.

Fold ½" Fold

Sew the binding strips to the left and right sides of the quilt, and finish them in the same way as the top and bottom bindings were finished.

Easy-Turn Finishing

This simple method is used to finish many of the accessories presented in this book. It also makes a quick, no-fuss finish for quilts and wall hangings.

1. Trim the backing and batting to the same size as the project top. Place the project top and backing right sides together, with the

backing as the top layer. Lay on the batting, carefully smoothing all layers, and pin.

2. Unless otherwise noted, sew around the outside raw edges with a ¼"-wide seam allowance. Leave an opening large enough for turning the project right side out.

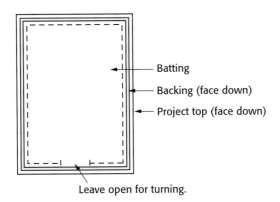

Leave open for turning.

3. Trim the excess seam allowance as necessary, clip the corners on the diagonal, and turn the project through the opening.

4. Press the project, and slipstitch the opening closed.

Throw-Pillow Finishing

Follow these steps to finish the throw-pillow projects.

1. Lay the pillow-top and pillow-back pieces right sides together. Sew ¼" all around the perimeter, leaving an opening large enough to insert the fiberfill or pillow form. Trim any excess seam allowance and clip the corners on the diagonal.

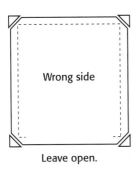

Leave open.

2. Turn the pillow right side out, press, stuff it with filler or a pillow form, and slipstitch the opening closed.

Pet Pillow-Cover Finishing

Each of the porch ensembles includes a pet bed that is simply a standard-size bed pillow with a decorative cover. The pillow-cover tops are styled to suit the season, but the finishing instructions for each one are the same.

1. Construct the pillow-cover top as instructed.

2. Layer the pillow-top backing, batting, and pillow-cover top; baste the layers together (see "Assembling the Layers" on page 14).

3. Secure the layers together as instructed for each pillow cover.

4. Refer to "Ties" on page 18 to make 6 ties from the strips indicated in the project directions. With right sides and raw edges together, center a tie on the upper edge of the pillow-cover top. Position a tie on each side of the center tie halfway between the center tie and the outer edge of the pillow-cover top. Place the remaining 3 ties on the right side of the pillow-cover back in corresponding positions. Baste the ties in place. Tie a knot in the unbasted end of each tie strip.

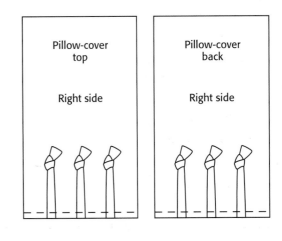

5. Refer to "Easy-Turn Finishing" on page 16 to stitch the pillow-cover front and pillow-cover back together along the side and bottom edges.

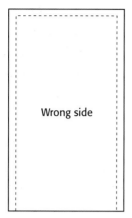

Wrong side

6. Refer to "Finishing the Edges" on page 15 to join the binding strips together. Cut one end at a 45° angle. Press the angled end under ¼". This will be the beginning of the strip. Press the binding strip in half lengthwise, wrong sides together, aligning the raw edges.

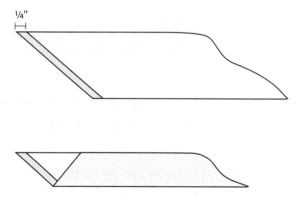

¼"

7. With right sides together and raw edges even, place the pressed-under end of the binding strip along the pillow-cover back upper edge. Begin stitching 2" from the binding end, and end stitching approximately 2" from the beginning of the binding strip, leaving the needle down in the fabric. Trim the end of the binding so it overlaps the beginning by 2". Tuck the cut end of the binding strip inside the diagonal fold. Be sure that the join is smooth on the long folded edge. Pin; then finish sewing the binding to the cover.

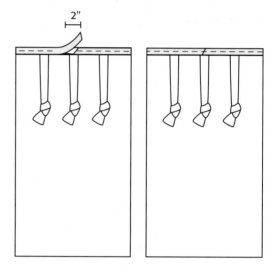

2"

8. Fold the binding to the inside of the pillow cover and whipstitch the folded edge in place (refer to "French Binding" on page 15).

Special Touches

General construction techniques for ties and piping are described here. Specific cutting and sewing requirements appear with the individual project instructions.

Ties

1. Fold each tie strip in half, wrong sides together, matching the long raw edges; press.

2. Open the strip; then refold the raw edges to meet at the crease and press.

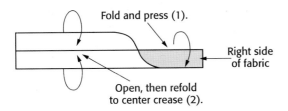

Fold and press (1).

Right side of fabric

Open, then refold to center crease (2).

3. Refold the strip along the center crease and topstitch close to the "double" folded edges.

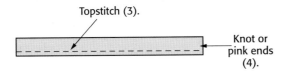

Topstitch (3).

Knot or pink ends (4).

Piping

1. Sew bias fabric strips end to end, right sides together, until you have achieved the required length for piping (refer to "French Binding" on page 15 to join the strips).

2. Center the cotton cording on the wrong side of the long fabric strip. Fold the fabric over the cording, aligning the raw edges, and use a zipper foot to machine baste next to the cording.

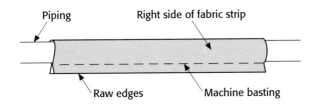

Piping

Right side of fabric strip

Raw edges

Machine basting

3. With right sides together and long raw edges aligned, follow the project instructions to pin the piping to the project. Overlap the end of the piping with the beginning of the piping ½". Trim away the excess. Pull the cording out of the end of the fabric tube and cut off ½". The ends of the cording should meet, and the fabric should extend ½" beyond one end of the cording.

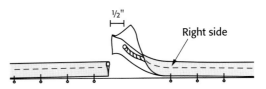

½"

Right side

4. Baste the piping in place, starting ½" from the beginning of the piping. As you approach the end, turn the excess fabric at the end of the piping under ¼". Wrap the turned-under edge around the beginning of the piping.

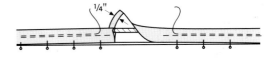

¼"

5. Continue basting until you are ½" beyond the point where you began basting.

GENERAL PAINTING INSTRUCTIONS

Most of the painting projects in this book are simple enough for a beginner to attempt, but if you're still apprehensive, consult with the professionals at your local craft or decorative painting supply shop.

For each project presented, a paint palette and materials list is given. Refer to the project photographs for design placement ideas.

Supplies

Brushes

You'll need brushes in several sizes and types to apply the paint to the project. Polyfoam brushes are ideal for painting base coats in large areas. I find that a 2", 1½", 1", and ½" are the most handy. For more detailed painting, you will need decorative paint brushes in the following types and sizes: #3 Round; #8, #12, and #14 Shader; #2 and #10/0 Liner.

Graphite Paper

Graphite paper is needed to transfer the pattern to the project. Make the lines clear enough to see, but light enough that the paint will cover the marks.

Miscellaneous Accessories

A paint palette is necessary for holding the paint. You can use a purchased palette, a disposable plastic plate, or even a clean meat tray. You will also need a brush basin or other receptacle to hold water for cleaning the brushes between colors, and paper towels for blotting brushes and for cleanup.

Paints

We use three brands of acrylic paints and all are generally available in local craft stores. Refer to the project instructions for specific paint colors and brands.

Sanding Supplies

Sand wood projects with a fine sanding disk before painting. Remove the sanding dust from the surface with a tack cloth. Do the final sanding with a brown paper bag.

Sealer

Set paint and ink with a matte-finish acrylic sealer.

Tape

Use Scotch Magic Tape to mask off borders and straight lines.

Tracing Paper

Trace the patterns in the book onto tracing paper.

Terms and Techniques

Base Coat

A base coat is a solid application of paint covering the surface or design. Two or three light coats are better than one heavy coat. Sand lightly between coats with a sanding disk or a brown paper bag. Remove sanding dust with a tack cloth. Allow paint to dry between coats, or before painting adjacent areas.

Shading and Highlighting

Shade and highlight by floating the color onto the base coat. Shade first, and then highlight. Shade with a color one value darker than the base coat. Highlight with one shade lighter than the base coat.

Sponging

In the sponging technique, paint is dabbed onto a surface with a sponge. Use a natural sponge. Let your eye tell you when you have covered the surface enough. Lightly dampen the sponge and squeeze out the excess water. Dip the sponge into the paint, blot it on a paper towel, and bounce the sponge up and down on the desired surface.

Taping

Use Scotch Magic Tape to mask off areas you do not want to be painted or to keep the painted line crisp. Paint; then remove the tape and let the paint dry.

Transferring Patterns

Check the pattern against the surface it will be applied to for correct size. If necessary, use a photocopy machine to reduce or enlarge the pattern. Trace the desired design onto tracing paper; then tape the design to the project surface. Slip graphite paper between the tracing paper and surface. Use a pen, pencil, or stylus to mark over the design lines and transfer the design to the surface.

Floating

Wet the brush and blot it on a paper towel until the shine is gone. Then dip about one-third of the brush in the paint and stroke back and forth on the palette until the color is blended. Pull the brush along the design areas to be highlighted or shaded until the colors are soft with no stop or start marks.

Penstitching

Mock stitching lines can be achieved with paint and a fine liner brush or with a fine-tip permanent marker. Let the painted design dry at least twenty-four hours before penstitching. Let the penstitched project dry twenty-four hours before sealing.

SPRING PORCH

>⋅+⋅-⋅O⋅-⋅+⋅<

The crocuses are up, the first robin has been sighted, and it's time to get your porch ready for enjoying the weather ahead. This coordinated ensemble proves just the right touch for welcoming spring to the neighborhood. Enjoy piecing a quilt, tablecloth, and chair back cover, each fresh with new-sprung blooms for you to enjoy. There's even a matching cover for a standard-size bed pillow that makes just the right spot for pets of all kinds to relax with you. When the stitching is done, pull out the paints and add a touch of whimsy to a host of accessories.

The Basic Flower Blocks

The following instructions explain how to construct the basic blocks that will be used to make the stitched projects in this ensemble. For the tablecloth and quilt outer border, only the head portion of the flower is used. The Whole Flower block is created by adding on to the Flower Head block. The directions for each project will tell how many Flower Head and/or Whole Flower blocks to make.

1. To make Strip Set A, alternately stitch together 2 identical dark-print and 3 background strips, each 1¼" wide. Begin and end with a background strip. Press the seams toward the dark-print strips. Cut the strip set into 1¼"-wide segments.

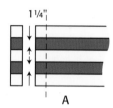

2. To make Strip Set B, stitch identical 2"-wide dark-print strips to each side of a 1¼"-wide medium-print strip. Press the seams toward the medium-print strip. Cut the strip set into 1¼"-wide segments.

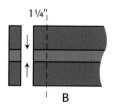

3. To make Strip Set C, stitch 1 gold, 2 identical medium-print, and 2 background strips, each 1¼" wide, together as shown. Press the seams toward the medium-print strips. Cut the strip set into 1¼"-wide segments.

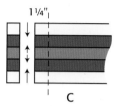

4. To make Strip Set D, stitch 1 medium green and 1 background strip, each 2" wide, together as shown. Press the seam toward the background strip. Cut the strip set into 1¼"-wide segments.

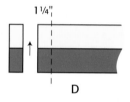

5. To make Strip Set E, stitch a 2¾"-wide medium green strip to a 1¼"-wide background strip as shown. Press the seam toward the medium green strip. Cut the strip set into 1¼"-wide segments.

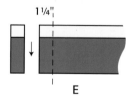

6. To make the Flower Head blocks, stitch the strip-set segments together as shown. For each flower head, you will need 2 A, 2 B, and 1 C segments with identical outer and inner petal fabrics. Press the seams in one direction.

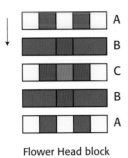

Flower Head block

7. To make the Whole Flower block, stitch a 2" x 4½" background strip to each side of the Flower Head block. Press the seams toward the background strips.

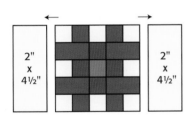

8. Stitch 2 D strip-set segments, 4 E strip-set segments, and 2 background 1¼" x 3½" strips as shown for the block leaves. Press the seams in the direction shown.

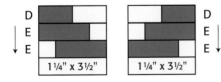

9. For the stem, stitch a 1¼" x 3½" dark green strip to 1 leaf unit. Press the seam toward the dark green strip. Stitch the remaining leaf unit to the stem-and-leaf unit as shown.

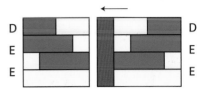

10. Stitch the complete stem-and-leaf unit to the flower head unit. Press the seam toward the stem-and-leaf unit.

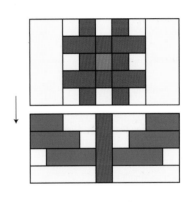

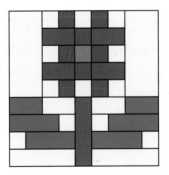

Whole Flower Block

QUILT

Finished Quilt Size: 59¼" x 74¼"
Finished Whole Flower Block Size: 6¾" x 6¾"
Finished Flower Head Block Size: 3¾" x 3¾"

Materials

42"-wide fabric

4⅜ yds. off-white solid for plain blocks, block backgrounds, inner borders, and outer borders

1 fat quarter *each* of 6 assorted dark prints for flower outer petals

1 fat quarter *each* of 3 assorted medium prints for flower inner petals

⅜ yd. gold print for flower centers

¼ yd. dark green print or solid for flower stems

⅝ yd. medium green print for flower leaves

Twin-size batting (72" x 90")

4 yds. fabric for backing

Cutting

All measurements include ¼"-wide seam allowances.

From the off-white solid, cut:
    31 squares, each 7¼" x 7¼", for quilt-center plain blocks
    32 squares, each 4¼" x 4¼", for border plain blocks
    2 strips, each 2" x 42", for block backgrounds
    8 strips, each 2" x 42"; crosscut to make 64 strips, each 2" x 4½", for block backgrounds
    2 strips, each 1¼" x 42", for block backgrounds
    30 strips, each 1¼" x 42"; crosscut to make:
        64 strips, each 1¼" x 3½", for block backgrounds
        48 strips, each 1¼" x 18", for block backgrounds
    3 strips, each 1¼" x 42", for inner side borders
    3 strips, each 2" x 42", for inner top and bottom borders
    7 strips, each 2" x 42", for outer borders

From *each* of the 6 assorted dark prints, cut:
    2 strips, each 1¼" x 42"; crosscut to make 4 strips, each 1¼" x 18", for flower outer petals
    2 strips, each 2" x 42"; crosscut to make 4 strips, each 2" x 18", for flower outer petals

From *each* of the 3 assorted medium prints, cut:
    4 strips, each 1¼" x 42"; crosscut to make 8 strips, each 1¼" x 18", for flower inner petals

From the gold print, cut:
    3 strips, each 1¼" x 42"; crosscut to make 6 strips, each 1¼" x 18", for flower centers

From the dark green print or solid, cut:
    3 strips, each 1¼" x 42"; crosscut to make 32 strips, each 1¼" x 3½", for flower stems

From the medium green print, cut:
    2 strips, each 2" x 42", for flower leaves
    4 strips, each 2¾" x 42", for flower leaves

From the backing fabric, cut:
    2 pieces, each 42" x 72"

Assembling the Quilt Top

Refer to "The Basic Flower Blocks" on pages 24–25 for steps 1–7.

1. Use the 1¼" x 18" off-white background strips and assorted dark-print strips to make 12 A strip sets. Make 2 A strip sets from each of the 6 assorted dark prints. Cut 64 identical *pairs* of 1¼"-wide segments (128 total).

2. Set aside four 1¼" x 18" strips from each of the 3 assorted medium prints to make the C strip sets. Use the 2" x 18" assorted dark-print strips and the remaining 1¼" x 18" assorted medium-print strips to make 12 B strip sets. Cut 64 identical pairs of 1¼"-wide segments (128 total).

3. Use the 1¼" x 18" gold, assorted medium-print strips that were set aside in step 2, and off-white background strips to make 6 C strip sets. Cut the strips into 64 segments, each 1¼" wide.

4. Make 2 of Strip Set D by using the 2" x 42" off-white background strips and medium green strips. Cut the strips into 64 segments, each 1¼" wide.

5. Make 4 of Strip Set E by using the medium green 2¾" x 42" strips and 1¼" x 42" off-white background strips. Cut the strips into 128 segments, each 1¼" wide.

6. Assemble 64 Flower Head blocks by using segments from Strip Sets A, B, and C. The outer and inner petal fabrics in each block *must be identical.* Set aside 32 Flower Head blocks for the middle border.

7. Assemble the remaining Flower Head blocks, the 2" x 4½" and 1¼" x 3½" off-white background strips, the 1¼" x 3½" dark green strips, and the segments from Strip Sets D and E into Whole Flower blocks. Make 32.

8. Arrange the Whole Flower blocks and 7¼" x 7¼" off-white plain blocks in 9 horizontal rows of 7 blocks each. Alternate the block position in each row as shown. Press the seams toward the plain blocks. Sew the rows together. Press the seam allowances in one direction.

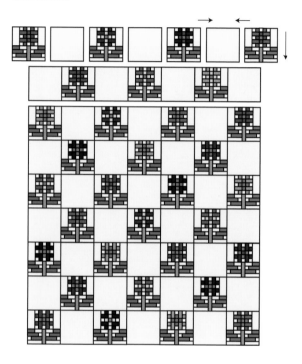

9. Stitch the off-white inner side border strips together end to end to make one long strip. From the long strip, cut 2 segments, each 1¼" x 65¾". Stitch the inner top and bottom border strips together end to end to make one long strip. From this strip, cut 2 segments, each 2" x 52¾". Refer to "Adding Borders" on page 12 to stitch the inner border strips to the quilt top.

10. To make the middle side borders, alternately stitch together nine 4¼" x 4¼" off-white plain blocks and 8 Flower Head blocks. Begin and end with a plain block. Press the seams toward the plain blocks. Make 2. To make the middle top and bottom borders,

alternately stitch together 8 Flower Head blocks and seven 4¼" x 4¼" plain blocks, beginning and ending with a Flower Head block. Press the seams toward the plain blocks. Make 2. Refer to "Adding Borders" on page 12 to stitch the middle border strips to the quilt top.

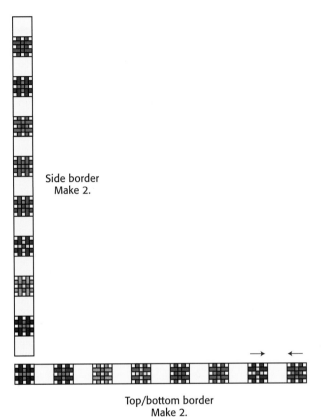

Side border
Make 2.

Top/bottom border
Make 2.

11. Stitch the outer border strips together end to end to make one long strip. From the long strip, cut 2 segments, each 2" x 71¾", for the outer side borders. Then cut 2 segments, each 2" x 59¼", for the outer top and bottom borders. Refer to "Adding Borders" on page 12 to stitch the outer borders to the quilt top.

Finishing the Quilt

1. Stitch the backing pieces together to make a 72" x 84" piece (see "Choosing Batting and Backing" on page 13). Trim the backing to 64" x 78".

2. Layer the backing, batting, and quilt top; baste the layers together (see "Assembling the Layers" on page 14).

3. Quilt as desired (see "Quilting" on page 14).

4. From the remaining scraps of medium print and dark print fat quarters, cut enough 2½"-wide strips to make 280" of binding strips. French bind the quilt edges (see "Finishing the Edges" on page 15).

TABLECLOTH

Finished Tablecloth Size: 36¾" x 36¾"
Finished Block Size: 6¾" x 6¾"

Materials

42"-wide fabric

1¾ yds. off-white solid for tablecloth center square, block backgrounds, inner border plain blocks, and outer borders

1 fat quarter *each* of 4 assorted dark prints for flower outer petals

1 fat quarter *each* of 3 assorted medium prints for flower inner petals

1 fat quarter of gold print for flower centers

1⅜ yds. flannel for backing

Cutting

All measurements include ¼"-wide seam allowances.

From the off-white solid, cut:

1 square, 26¾" x 26¾", for tablecloth center

18 strips, each 1¼" x 18", for block backgrounds

16 squares, each 4¼" x 4¼", for inner border plain blocks

2 strips, each 2" x 34¼", for outer side borders

2 strips, each 2" x 37¼", for outer top and bottom borders

From *each* of the 4 assorted dark prints, cut:

2 strips, 1¼" x 18", for flower outer petals

2 strips, 2" x 18", for flower outer petals

From 2 of the 3 assorted medium prints, cut from each:

3 strips, each 1¼" x 18", for flower inner petals

From the remaining medium print, cut:

4 strips, each 1¼" x 18", for flower inner petals

From the gold print, cut:

3 strips, each 1¼" x 18", for block centers

From the flannel backing fabric, cut:

1 square, 40" x 40"

Assembling the Tablecloth

Refer to "The Basic Flower Blocks" on pages 24–25 for steps 1–5.

1. Use the 1¼" x 18" off-white background strips and assorted dark-print strips to make 4 A strip sets. Make 1 A strip set from each of the 4 assorted dark prints. Cut 16 identical pairs of 1¼"-wide segments (32 total).

2. Use the 2" x 18" assorted dark-print strips and the 1¼" x 18" assorted medium-print strips to make 4 B strip sets. Make 1 B strip set from each of the 4 assorted dark prints and 3 medium prints; use 1 medium print twice. Cut 16 identical *pairs* of 1¼"-wide segments (32 total).

3. Use the 1¼" x 18" gold, assorted medium-print, and off-white background strips to make 3 C strip sets. From each of 2 of the C strip sets, cut four 1¼"-wide segments (8 total). From the remaining C strip set, cut 8 segments, each 1¼" wide.

4. Assemble 16 Flower Head blocks by using segments from Strip Sets A, B, and C. The outer and inner petal fabrics in each block *must be identical.*

5. To make the inner side borders, alternately stitch together 3 Flower Head blocks and four 4¼" x 4¼" off-white plain blocks. Begin and end with a plain block. Make 2.

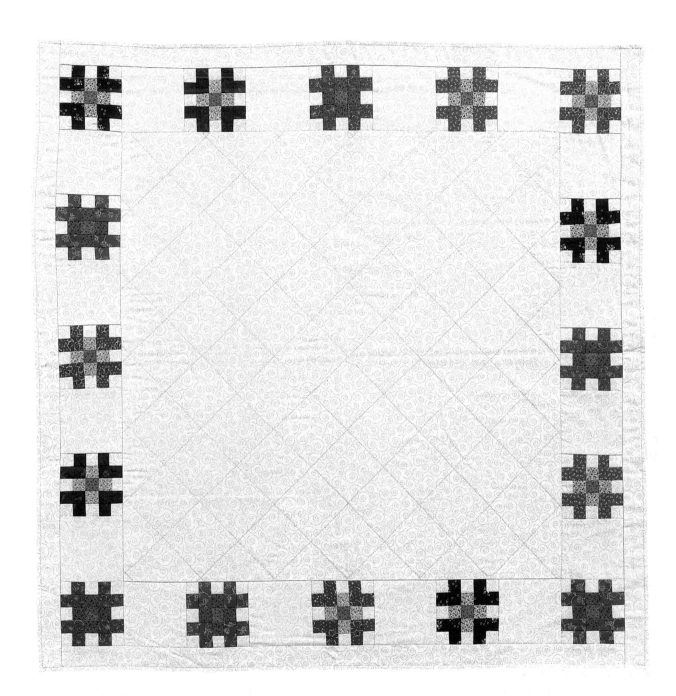

To make the inner top and bottom borders, alternately stitch together 5 Flower Head blocks and four 4¼" x 4¼" plain blocks. Begin and end with a Flower Head block. Make 2. Refer to "Adding Borders" on page 12 to stitch the inner and outer borders to the tablecloth top.

Finishing the Tablecloth

1. Refer to "Easy-Turn Finishing" on page 16 to stitch the tablecloth top and flannel backing together.
2. Quilt as desired (see "Quilting" on page 14).

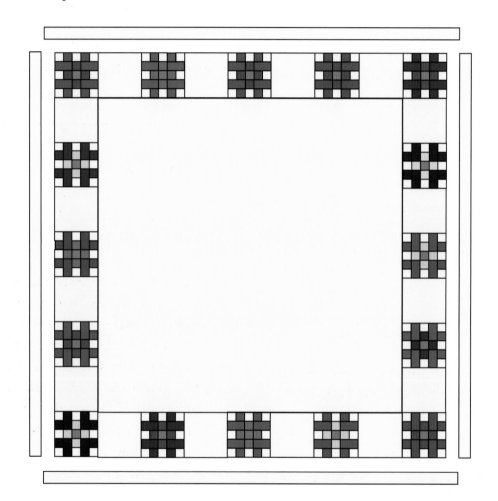

CHAIR PAD

Materials

42"-wide fabric*

½ yd. medium green print for chair pad
1 yd. off-white solid for ruffle
Pattern tracing paper
½ yd. high-loft bonded batting
4½ yds. off-white, 1"-wide grosgrain ribbon for ties
Polyester fiberfill (optional)

*The materials given are the approximate amount needed to make 1 chair pad. To determine the exact yardage, follow step 1 below to make the pattern; then determine the yardage needed to cut 2 chair pad pieces for each cushion desired.

Cutting and Assembling the Chair Pad

Use ½" seam allowances unless noted otherwise.

1. Lay the pattern tracing paper over the chair seat and trace around the outer edges to make a pattern. Add ½" to all of the edges for seam allowance. Using the pattern as a guide, cut 1 piece each from the medium green print and batting for the chair pad top. Cut each piece 2" to 3" larger all the way around the pattern. From the medium green print, cut another piece along the pattern lines for the chair pad bottom.

2. With the right side facing up, lay the chair pad top piece over the batting piece. Quilt as desired (see "Quilting" on page 14). Lay the pattern on top of the quilted piece and follow the pattern lines to cut the top to size. Lay the quilted top on the chair. Pin-mark the front and back tie placement points.

3. To make the ruffle, measure around the pattern outer edges. Cut enough 6½"-wide strips from the off-white fabric to equal twice the measured distance around the pattern edges. Stitch the strips together end to end to make one long strip. Press the seams open.

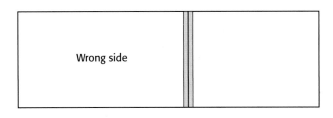

4. Measure the area between the back tie placement points on the quilted top. From the pieced ruffle strip, cut a piece twice the length measured. Press the ends of the long and short ruffle strips under ½" and stitch in place. Press each ruffle strip in half lengthwise, wrong sides together. Sew a row of basting stitches ⅛" from the raw edges of each strip, leaving long thread tails at the beginning and end.

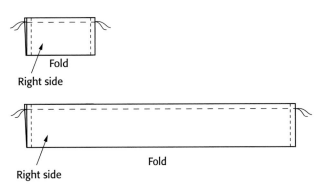

5. Gather the short ruffle strip to fit between the back tie placement points. Gather the long ruffle strip to fit around the remaining edges of the quilted top. With raw edges matching, pin the ruffle strips to the right side of the quilted top. Distribute the gathers evenly.

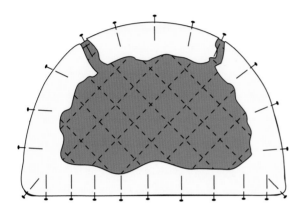

6. Cut the grosgrain ribbon into 4 equal pieces. Fold each piece in half so the raw ends are aligned. Pin the back ties into place *between* *the pad and ruffle*. Pin the front ties in place on top of the ruffle. Baste around the chair pad top outer edges.

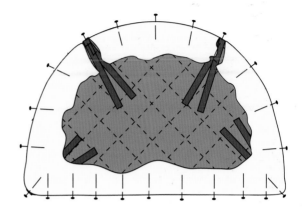

7. With right sides together, stitch the chair pad bottom to the top, keeping the tie ends away from the seam line. Leave an opening for turning along the back edge. Turn the chair pad to the right side. If desired, stuff the pad with fiberfill until it is the desired firmness. Slipstitch the opening closed.

CHAIR BACK COVER

Finished Cover Size: 15¾" x 21½"*
Finished Block Size: 6¾" x 6¾"

The cover size can be adjusted by changing the width and or length of the vertical and horizontal sashing strips.

Materials

42"-wide fabric

⅝ yd. off-white solid for block backgrounds and sashing strips

⅛ yd. *each* or scraps of 4 assorted dark prints for flower outer petals

⅛ yd. *each* or scraps of 2 medium prints for flower inner petals

⅛ yd. or scrap of gold print for flower centers

¼ yd. or scrap of medium green print for flower leaves

⅛ yd. or scrap of dark green print for flower stems

20" x 25" piece of low-loft batting

¾ yd. fabric for backing

3 yds. off-white, 1"-wide grosgrain ribbon

Cutting

All measurements include ¼"-wide seam allowances.

From the off-white solid, cut:

7 strips, each 1¼" x 42"; crosscut to make:

16 strips, each 1¼" x 12", for block backgrounds

8 strips, each 1¼" x 3½", for block backgrounds

6 strips, each 1¼" x 7¼", for vertical sashing strips

2 strips, each 2" x 42"; crosscut to make:

2 strips, each 2" x 12", for block backgrounds

8 strips, each 2" x 4½", for block backgrounds

2 strips, each 2½" x 42"; crosscut to make 4 strips, each 2½" x 16¼", for horizontal sashing strips

From *each* of the 4 assorted dark prints, cut:

2 strips, each 1¼" x 12", for flower outer petals

2 strips, each 2" x 12", for flower outer petals

From *each* of the 2 medium prints, cut:

4 strips, each 1¼" x 12", for flower inner petals

From the gold print, cut:

2 strips, 1¼" x 12", for flower centers

From the medium green print, cut:

1 strip, 2" x 12", for flower leaves

2 strips, each 2¾" x 12", for flower leaves

From the dark green print, cut:

4 strips, each 1¼" x 3½", for flower stems

From the backing fabric, cut:

1 piece, 20" x 25"

Assembling the Chair Back Cover

Refer to "The Basic Flower Blocks" on pages 24–25 for steps 1–6.

1. Use the 1¼" x 12" off-white background strips and assorted dark-print strips to make 4 A strip sets. Make 1 A strip set from each of the 4 assorted dark prints. Cut 1 identical pair of 1¼"-wide segments from each strip set (8 total).

2. Use the 2" x 12" assorted dark-print strips and the 1¼" x 12" medium-print strips to make 4 B strip sets. Make 1 B strip set from each of the 4 assorted dark prints; use each medium print twice. Cut 1 identical *pair* of 1¼"-wide segments from each strip set (8 total).

3. Use the 1¼" x 12" gold, medium-print, and off-white background strips to make 2 C strip sets. Make 1 C strip set from each medium print. Cut each strip set into 2 segments, each 1¼" wide (4 total).

4. Make 1 D strip set by using the 2" x 12" medium green strip and a 1¼" x 12" off-white background strip. Cut the strip into 8 segments, each 1¼" wide.

5. Make 2 E strip sets by using the 2¾" x 12" medium green strips and the 1¼" x 12" off-white background strips. From the strip sets, cut 16 segments, each 1¼" wide.

6. Assemble 4 Whole Flower blocks by using segments from Strip Sets A, B, C, D, and E; the 2" x 4½" and 1¼" x 3½" off-white background strips; and the 1¼" x 3½" dark green strips. The outer and inner petal fabrics in each block *must be identical*.

7. Alternately stitch together 2 blocks and 3 vertical sashing strips, beginning and ending with a sashing strip. Stitch a horizontal sashing strip to the top and bottom of the block unit. Make 2.

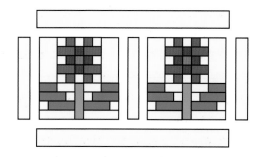

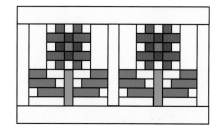

Make 2.

8. Stitch the block units together as shown with the flower heads facing each other.

Finishing the Chair Back Cover

1. Lay the chair back cover over the batting, right side up.

2. Quilt as desired (see "Quilting" on page 14), leaving the sashing strips unquilted.

3. Refer to "Easy-Turn Finishing" on page 16 to stitch the quilted top and backing together. Quilt the sashing strips.

4. Cut the grosgrain ribbon into 8 equal pieces. Press one end of each piece under 1". Position the pressed-under end of each tie 1" from the cover edges as shown. Stitch the ties in place by using an X-stitch formation for added strength. Tie the ribbon raw ends in a knot.

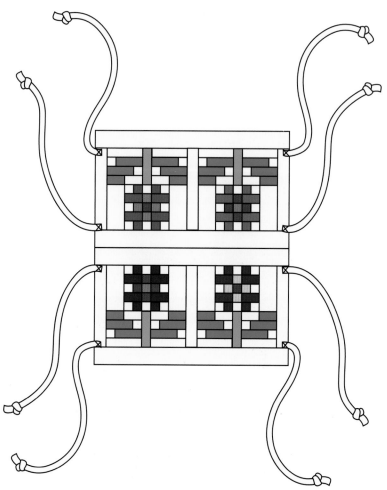

PET PILLOW

Finished Pillow-Cover Size: 25½" x 36½"
Finished Block Size: 8½" x 8½"

Materials
42"-wide fabric

1⅜ yds. off-white solid for plain blocks, block backgrounds, and borders

⅛ yd. *each* or scraps of 5 assorted dark prints for flower outer petals

⅛ yd. *each* or scraps of 5 assorted medium prints for flower inner petals

⅛ yd. or scrap of gold print for flower centers

¼ yd. medium green print for flower leaves

⅛ yd. or scrap of dark green print for flower stems

29" x 40" piece of batting

1 yd. muslin for pillow-top backing

1 yd. fabric for pillow back

Standard-size pillow

Cutting

All measurements include ¼"-wide seam allowances.

From the off-white solid, cut:
　4 squares, each 9" x 9", for plain blocks
　6 strips, each 1¼" x 42"; crosscut to make:
　　25 strips, each 1¼" x 6", for block backgrounds
　　10 strips, each 1¼" x 3½", for block backgrounds
　　1 strip, 1¼" x 30", for block backgrounds
　2 strips, each 2" x 42"; crosscut to make:
　　1 strip, 2" x 15", for block backgrounds
　　10 strips, each 2" x 4½", for block backgrounds

5 strips, each 1⅜" x 42"; crosscut to make:
　10 strips, each 1⅜" x 7¼", for block side borders
　10 strips, each 1⅜" x 9", for block top and bottom borders
2 strips, each 6" x 26", for pillow-cover top and bottom borders

From *each* of the 5 assorted dark prints, cut:
　2 strips, each 1¼" x 6", for flower outer petals
　2 strips, each 2" x 6", for flower outer petals

From *each* of the 5 assorted medium prints, cut:
　3 strips, each 1¼" x 6", for flower inner petals

From the gold print, cut:
　5 strips, each 1¼" x 6", for flower centers

From the medium green print, cut:
　1 strip, 2" x 15", for flower leaves
　1 strip, 2¾" x 30", for flower leaves

From the dark green print, cut:
　5 strips, each 1¼" x 3½", for flower stems

From the muslin, cut:
　1 piece, 29" x 40", for pillow-top backing

From the pillow-back fabric, cut:
　1 piece, 26" x 37"

Assembling the Pet Pillow

Refer to "The Basic Flower Blocks" on pages 24–25 for steps 1–6.

1. Use the 1¼" x 6" off-white background strips and assorted dark-print strips to make 5 A strip sets. Make 1 A strip set from each of the 5 assorted dark prints. Cut 2 identical pairs of 1¼"-wide segments from each strip set (10 total).

2. Use the 2" x 6" assorted dark-print strips and the 1¼" x 6" assorted medium-print strips to make 5 B strip sets. Make 1 B strip set from each of the 5 assorted dark prints and medium prints. Cut 2 identical pairs of 1¼"-wide segments from each strip set (10 total).

3. Use the 1¼" x 6" gold, assorted medium-print, and off-white background strips to make 5 C strip sets. Make 1 C strip set from each medium print. Cut 1 segment from each strip set, each 1¼" wide (5 total).

4. Make 1 D strip set by using the 2" x 15" medium green strip and off-white back-

ground strip. Cut the strip into 10 segments, each 1¼" wide.

5. Make 1 E strip set by using the 2¾" x 30" medium green strip and 1¼" x 30" off-white background strip. From the strip set, cut 20 segments, each 1¼" wide.

6. Assemble 5 Whole Flower blocks by using segments from Strip Sets A, B, C, D, and E; the 2" x 4½" and 1¼" x 3½" off-white background strips; and the 1¼" x 3½" dark green strips. The outer and inner petal fabrics in each block *must be identical*.

7. Stitch the block side border strips to the sides of each block. Press the seam allowance toward the border. Stitch the block top and bottom border strips to the top and bottom of each block. Press the seam allowance toward the border.

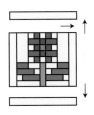

8. Arrange the blocks and the 9" x 9" off-white plain blocks in 3 horizontal rows of 3 blocks each. Alternate the block position in each row as shown. Sew the blocks together into rows. Press the seam allowances in opposite directions from row to row. Stitch the rows

together. Press the seam allowances in one direction.

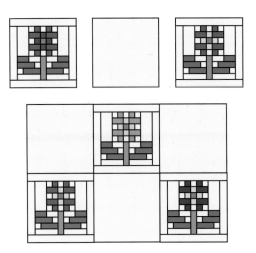

9. Stitch the off-white, 6" x 26" top and bottom borders to the top and bottom edges of the pillow cover.

10. Refer to "Pet Pillow-Cover Finishing" on page 17 to finish constructing the pillow cover. Quilt the layers together as desired.

11. Insert pillow into cover and tie corresponding ties together into a bow.

WATERING CAN AND FLOWERPOT

Acrylic Paint Palette

Delta Ceramcoat: Metal Primer, #2131 Nightfall Blue, #2095 English Yew Green, #2495 Cinnamon, #2506 Black, #2492 Oyster White, #2435 Trail Tan, #2029 Caucasian Flesh, #2063 Spice Tan, #2093 Pigskin

Plaid FolkArt: #420 Linen

Materials

Galvanized watering can and flowerpot
Vinegar
Paintbrushes: #8 and #14 Flat, #10/0 Liner
Matte-finish acrylic spray sealer

Surface Preparation

1. Wash the watering can and flowerpot with a 50 percent vinegar/50 percent water mixture. Rinse with clean water; dry with a clean cloth.
2. Follow the metal primer instructions to prime the watering can and flowerpot outer surfaces.
3. Enlarge or reduce the flower pattern on page 122 to fit the watering can and flowerpot.

Painting the Designs

1. Refer to the photo to base coat the flowerpot as follows: upper portion, Nightfall Blue; first stripe, Linen; second stripe, English Yew Green; third stripe, Nightfall Blue; lower portion, Linen. Paint the stripes on the watering can with Nightfall Blue and Linen.
2. Transfer the flower pattern from step 3 of "Surface Preparation" and the bee pattern on page 122 to the flowerpot and watering can.
3. Paint the flowers on the flowerpot and watering can as follows: outer flower petals—Nightfall Blue, Cinnamon, or Black; inner flower petals—Oyster White, Trail Tan, or Caucasian Flesh; flower centers Spice Tan; leaves and stems English Yew Green.
4. On the flowerpot and watering can, paint the bee bodies with Pigskin and the stripes with Black. For the wings, float with Oyster White and shade close to the body with Black. Use Black and a liner brush to paint the legs and feelers.
5. With Black, penstitch around the outer edges of the entire flower. Penstitch the bee "buzz" lines.
6. Follow the manufacturer's instructions to apply several coats of sealer to the painted surfaces.

PAPIER-MÂCHÉ BUG KEEPER

Acrylic Paint Palette

Delta Ceramcoat: #2095 English Yew Green, #2492 Oyster White, #2506 Black, #2093 Pigskin

Materials

10½"(H) x 8"(W) x 4"(D) papier-mâché box with attached lid, handle, and closure
Matte-finish acrylic spray sealer
Double-sided adhesive tape
Two 7" x 7" pieces of fine-gauge metal screening fabric
Paintbrushes: #8 and #14 Flat, #10/0 Liner
.03 mm black permanent marker

Surface Preparation

1. Center and cut a 6" x 5½" opening on the box front and back.
2. Apply acrylic sealer to the outside surfaces of the box. Let dry.
3. Working inside the box, apply double-sided tape close to the opening edges. Place the screening pieces over the taped edges of each opening and press in place to secure.

Painting the Design

1. Apply a base coat of English Yew Green to the box, leaving ¼" unpainted around screen. Paint a thin line around the unpainted area with Black.
2. Transfer the bee design on page 122 to the box as desired. Paint the bee bodies with Pigskin and the stripes with Black. For the wings, float with Oyster White and shade close to the body with Black. Use the permanent marker to draw the legs and feelers.
3. Follow the manufacturer's instructions to apply several coats of sealer to the painted surfaces.

BARK CLOTH QUILT

Finished Quilt Size: 43¼" x 59"
Finished Block Size: 4½" x 4½"

Materials
42"-wide fabric

2½ yds. *total* of assorted floral bark cloth prints
    for blocks and binding*
1½ yds. dark blue bark cloth for sashing strips
    and side borders*
3 yds. fabric for backing
White pearl cotton
Tapestry needle

*Bark cloth is a medium-weight, 100 percent–
cotton, textured fabric that resembles tapa cloth.
(Tapa cloth is made in the Pacific islands from
pounded bark.) If you cannot find bark cloth, substitute home decorating fabrics.*

Cutting

*All measurements include ¼"-wide seam
allowances.*

From the assorted floral bark cloth prints, cut:
    88 squares, each 4½" x 4½", for blocks
From the dark blue bark cloth, cut:
    25 strips, each 1¾" x 42"; crosscut to make:
        77 strips, each 1¾" x 4½", for vertical
            sashing strips
        12 strips, each 1¾" x 41¼", for horizon-
            tal sashing strips
From the backing fabric, cut:
    2 pieces, each 42" x 47"

Quilt Top Assembly

1. To make the block rows, alternately stitch
together 8 blocks and 7 vertical sashing
strips, beginning and ending with a block.
Press the seam allowances toward the sashing
strips. Make 11.

2. Beginning and ending with a horizontal sashing strip, stitch the block rows and sashing strips together. Press the seam allowances toward the sashing strips.

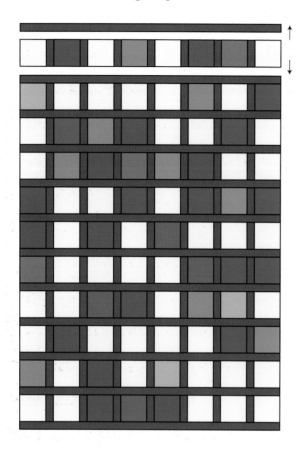

3. Sew the remaining 1¾" x 42" strips together end to end to make one long strip. From the long strip, cut 2 strips, each 1¾" x 59½", for the side borders. Refer to "Adding Borders" on page 12 to stitch the borders to the quilt sides.

Finishing the Quilt

1. Refer to "Choosing Batting and Backing" on page 13 to stitch the backing pieces together along the long edges to make 1 piece 47" x 84". Trim the pieced backing to 47" x 63".

2. Layer the backing and quilt top; baste the layers together (see "Assembling the Layers" on page 14).

3. Using the pearl cotton and tapestry needle, cross-stitch around the edges of each block as shown, going through all layers.

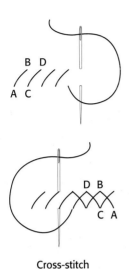

Cross-stitch

4. From the remaining floral bark cloth scraps, cut enough 2½"-wide strips to equal 210" when stitched together. French bind the quilt edges (see "Finishing the Edges" on page 15).

QUICK TO STITCH

BARK CLOTH PILLOWS

Finished Size: 14" x 14" and 16" x 16"

Materials*

42"-wide fabric

⅝ yd. cream floral bark cloth
¼ yd. red floral or plaid bark cloth
⅝ yd. fabric for pillow backs
Polyester fiberfill

Materials given are for both pillows.

Cutting

All measurements include ¼"-wide seam allowances.

From the cream floral bark cloth, cut:
   1 square, 14" x 14", for 16" pillow center square
   1 square, 12" x 12", for 14" pillow center square

From the red bark cloth, cut:
   3 strips, each 1¾" x 42"; crosscut to make:
      2 strips, each 1¾" x 14", for 16" pillow side borders
      2 strips, each 1¾" x 16½", for 16" pillow top and bottom borders
      2 strips, each 1¾" x 12", for 14" pillow side borders
      2 strips, each 1¾" x 14½", for 14" pillow top and bottom borders

From the backing fabric, cut:
   1 square, 16½" x 16½", for 16" pillow back
   1 square, 14½" x 14½", for 14" pillow back

Assembling the Pillows

1. For each pillow, refer to "Adding Borders" on page 12 to stitch the borders to the center square.
2. Refer to "Throw-Pillow Finishing" on page 17 to finish the pillows.

SUMMER PORCH

✥━◆━◇━◆━✥

Smell the salt air. Hear the waves swooshing against the sand. This ensemble will take you back to the beach, where your only worry was falling asleep in the sun. Create your own vacation spot at home with a lap throw that's also perfect for use as a cloth for a picnic lunch; pillows that wait for sleepy heads to rest upon them; and a plethora of accessories sure to put you in the mood for kicking back and relaxing. To be sure your projects stand up to the rigors of summer living, select a fabric such as canvas that's sturdy enough for the weather's temperament.

LAP THROW

Finished Lap Throw Size: 46" x 62"
Finished Block Size: 8" x 8"

Materials
42"-wide fabric*

1½ yds. red wide-striped canvas for blocks and
pieced binding

1⅜ yds. red medium-striped canvas for blocks
and pieced binding

⅞ yd. blue medium-striped canvas for blocks
and pieced binding

1¾ yds. red-and-blue striped canvas for border
and pieced binding

3¼ yds. canvas for backing

Pearl cotton or yarn for tying

**Because canvas is heavy, this quilt does not require
batting. If you choose to make your quilt top from
traditional quilting cotton, you will need a twin-
size piece of batting (72" x 90").*

Cutting

*All measurements include ¼"-wide seam
allowances.*

From the red wide-striped canvas, cut:
4 strips, each 8½" x 42"; crosscut to make 16
squares, each 8½" x 8½", for blocks

From the red medium-striped canvas, cut:
3 strips, each 8½" x 42"; crosscut to make 12
squares, each 8½" x 8½", for blocks

From the blue medium-striped canvas, cut:
2 strips, each 8½" x 42"; crosscut to make 7
squares, each 8½" x 8½", for blocks

From the canvas for backing, cut:
2 pieces, each 42" x 58½"

Assembling the Lap Throw

1. Stitch the 8½" striped squares into 7 horizontal rows of 5 blocks each as shown. Press
   the seam allowances in opposite directions
   from row to row. Stitch the rows together.
   Press the seam allowances in one direction.

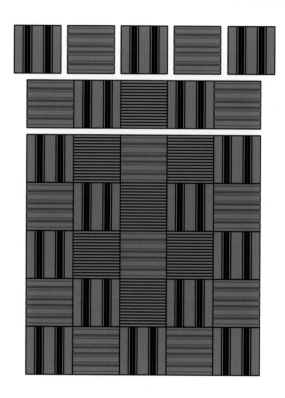

2. Refer to "Finishing the Edges" on page 15 to
   make 208" of 3½"-wide bias strips from
   the red-and-blue striped fabric. Join the
   strips together, matching the pattern. From
   the long strip, cut 2 segments, each 3½" x
   56½", for the side borders, and 2 segments,
   each 3½" x 46½", for the top and bottom
   borders.

3. Refer to "Adding Borders" on page 12 to carefully pin and stitch the borders to the quilt top. Make sure not to stretch the bias edges.

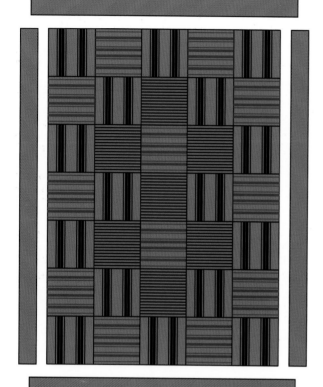

Finishing the Lap Throw

1. Refer to "Choosing Batting and Backing" on page 13 to stitch the backing pieces together along the long edges to make 1 piece, 58½" x 84". Trim the pieced backing to 50" x 66".

2. Lay the backing and top, right sides together; baste the layers together (see "Assembling the Layers" on page 14).

3. Refer to "Securing the Layers" on page 14 and use the pearl cotton or yarn to hand tie the layers together at the corners of each block.

4. Refer to "Finishing the Edges" on page 15 to cut the remaining block and border fabrics into 2½"-wide bias strips. Randomly piece the strips together to measure 220". French bind the quilt edges.

THROW PILLOWS

Finished Plain Pillow Size: 12" x 12"
Finished Flanged Pillow Size: 17" x 17"
Finished Block Size: 3" x 3"

Materials*
42"-wide fabric

¼ yd. *each* of 2 striped canvas prints for blocks
⅜ yd. coordinating striped canvas print for flanges
⅝ yd. striped canvas print for backing
Bag of polyester fiberfill

Materials given are for both pillows.

Cutting

All measurements include ¼"-wide seam allowances.

FOR THE PLAIN PILLOW

From *each* of the 2 striped canvas prints for blocks, cut:
  1 strip, 3½" x 42"; crosscut into 8 squares, each 3½" x 3½", for blocks
From the backing fabric, cut:
  1 square, 12½" x 12½"

FOR THE FLANGED PILLOW

From *each* of the 2 striped canvas prints for blocks, cut:
  1 strip, 3½" x 42"; crosscut to make 8 squares, each 3½" x 3½", for blocks

From the coordinating striped canvas print, cut:
  2 strips, each 3" x 12½", for side flanges
  2 strips, each 3" x 17½", for top and bottom flanges
From the backing fabric, cut:
  1 square, 17½" x 17½"

Assembling the Pillows

1. *To make the plain pillow,* stitch the 3½" striped squares into 4 rows of 4 blocks each as shown. Press the seam allowances in opposite directions from row to row. Stitch the rows together. Press the seam allowances in one direction.

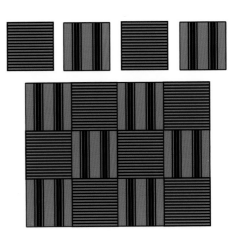

2. Refer to "Throw-Pillow Finishing" on page 17 to complete the pillow.

3. *To make the flanged pillow,* stitch the 3½" striped squares into 4 rows of 4 blocks each as shown for the plain pillow. Press the seam allowances in opposite directions from row to row. Stitch the rows together. Press the seam allowances in one direction.

4. Stitch the side flange strips to the pillow-top sides. Press the seam allowances toward the flange strips. Stitch the top and bottom flange strips to the top and bottom edges of the pillow top. Press the seam allowances toward the flange strips.

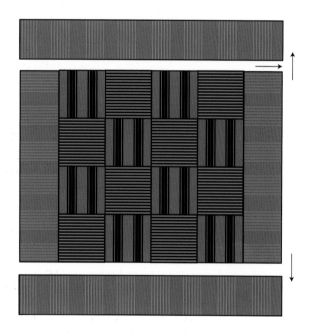

5. Place the backing and pieced pillow-top right sides together. Sew ¼" all around the perimeter, leaving an opening for turning. Clip the corners on the diagonal. Turn the pillow right side out and press. Stitch in the ditch of the seam that joins the flange strips to the pillow top, leaving the seam above the opening unstitched.

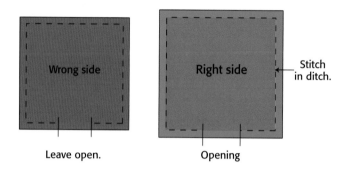

6. Stuff the pillow center with fiberfill until you reach the desired firmness. Machine stitch the flange opening closed. Slipstitch the pillow opening closed by hand.

PET PILLOW

Finished Pillow-Cover Size: 25" x 33"
Finished Block Size: 4" x 4"

Materials
42"-wide fabric

⅜ yd. red wide-striped canvas for blocks

1⅛ yds. red narrow-striped canvas for blocks, borders, ties, and binding

¼ yd. blue-and-red striped canvas for blocks

29" x 37" piece of batting

1 yd. muslin for pillow-top backing

1 yd. canvas for pillow back

Pearl cotton or yarn for tying

Standard-size pillow

Cutting

All measurements include ¼"-wide seam allowances.

From the red wide-striped canvas, cut:

2 strips, each 4½" x 42"; crosscut to make 16 squares, each 4½" x 4½", for blocks

From the red narrow-striped canvas, cut:

2 strips, each 4½" x 42"; crosscut to make 12 squares, each 4½" x 4½", for blocks

2 strips, each 3" x 28½", for side borders

2 strips, each 3" x 25½", for top and bottom borders

6 strips, each 2" x 18", for ties

2 strips, each 2½" x 42", for binding

From the blue-and-red striped canvas, cut:

7 squares, each 4½" x 4½", for blocks

From the muslin, cut:

1 piece, 29" x 37", for pillow-top backing

From the canvas for the pillow back, cut:

1 piece, 25½" x 33½"

Assembling the Pet Pillow Cover

1. Stitch the 4½" striped squares into 7 horizontal rows of 5 blocks each as shown. Press the seam allowances for each row in the opposite direction as the previous row. Stitch the rows together. Press the seam allowances in one direction.

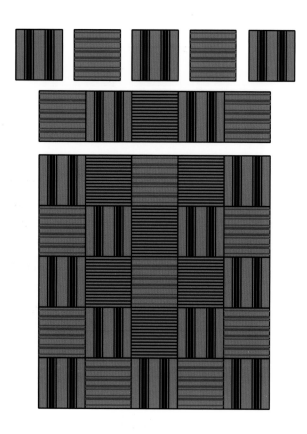

2. Refer to "Adding Borders" on page 12 to stitch the borders to the pillow-cover top.
3. Refer to "Pet Pillow-Cover Finishing" on page 17 to finish constructing the pillow cover, tying the layers together with the yarn or pearl cotton where indicated.

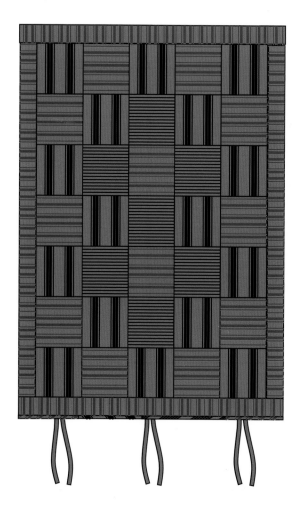

4. Insert pillow into cover and tie corresponding ties together into a bow.

FABRIC BASKET

Finished Size: Approximately 9½" x 9½"

Materials

42"-wide fabric

⅝ yd. print fabric of your choice for outer basket and ties

⅝ yd. coordinating solid for lining

13⅞" x 13⅞" square of batting

13⅞" x 13⅞" square of template plastic

90/14 sewing machine needle

Cutting

All measurements include ¼"-wide seam allowances.

From the print fabric, cut:

    1 square, 15" x 15", for outer basket

    8 strips, each 2" x 13", for ties

From the coordinating solid, cut:

    1 square, 15" x 15", for lining

Assembling the Basket

1. Refer to "Ties" on page 18 to make the ties.
2. Draw a 2½" square in each corner of the template plastic square. Cut out the squares.

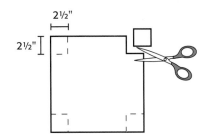

3. Press the raw edges of the outer basket and lining fabric squares under ½". Press under opposing sides first; then press under the remaining 2 edges.

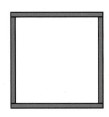

4. Layer the basket pieces in the following order: outer basket square, right side down; batting; template plastic; and lining square, right side up. Pin the edges together and trim away any batting or template plastic that is showing.

5. On the lining square, measure and draw a line 2¾" in from each outer edge.

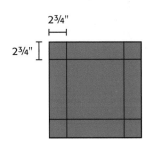

6. Insert one end of each tie strip between the batting and template plastic layers ½" in from the outer edge as shown. With the 90/14 needle in the machine, stitch around the perimeter, ⅛" from the edges. Backstitch over each tie strip to reinforce it. Then stitch over the drawn lines that are 2¾" in from each outer edge.

7. Cut the ends of each tie at an angle. To form the basket, tie the tie strips at each corner together into a bow. This will draw the sides up and a pleat will form in each corner.

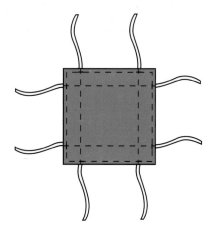

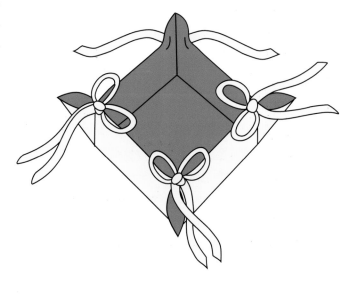

PLACE MATS, NAPKINS, AND NAPKIN RINGS

Finished Place Mat Size: 15" x 9"
Finished Napkin Size: 12" x 12"

Materials*
42"-wide fabric

1 yd. print fabric of your choice for place mat front and binding

⅝ yd. coordinating print for place mat backing

⅞ yd. each of 2 coordinating prints for napkins, napkin lining, and napkin rings

⅝ yd. cotton batting

4 clear plastic shower curtain rings

Materials given will make 4 sets.

Cutting

All measurements include ¼"-wide seam allowances.

From the place mat front and binding print, cut:

4 rectangles, each 10½" x 16½", for place mat front

6 strips, each 2½" x 42", for binding

From the coordinating print for place mat backing, cut:

4 rectangles, each 10½" x 16½"

From *each* of the 2 coordinating prints for napkins, cut:

4 squares, each 12½" x 12½", for napkins and napkin linings

2 strips, each 2" x 22", for napkin rings

From the cotton batting, cut:

4 rectangles, each 10½" x 16½"

Assembling the Place Mats, Napkins, and Napkin Rings

1. *To make each place mat,* layer the pieces in the following order: backing, wrong side up; batting; place mat front, right side up. Hand or machine quilt a 2½"-wide diagonal grid design on the place mat.

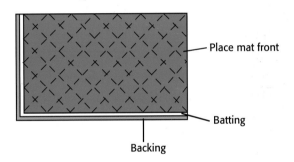

Place mat front

Batting

Backing

2. Square up and trim the place mat to 9½" x 15½".

3. French bind the place mat edges (see "Finishing the Edges" on page 15).

4. *To make each napkin,* place 2 different coordinating napkin squares right sides together. Using a ¼" seam allowance, stitch around the napkin edges, leaving an opening for turning. Turn the napkin to the right side, press, and topstitch close to the napkin edges.

5. *To make each napkin ring,* press each 2" x 22" napkin-ring strip end under ½". Fold the strip in half lengthwise, right sides together. Stitch ⅛" from the long edge. Turn the tube right side out.

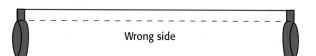

Wrong side

6. Open a shower curtain ring. Insert one end of the ring into the fabric tube and gather the fabric over the ring. Close the shower curtain ring.

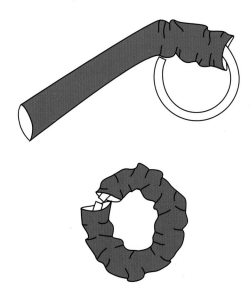

BEACH CHAIR CATCHALL

Finished Catchall Size: 9" x 14"

Materials

42"-wide fabric

1 yd. fabric of your choice for catchall body and
  pocket
2 yds. ½"-wide grosgrain ribbon

Cutting

*All measurements include ¼"-wide seam
allowances.*

From the fabric, cut:
  2 strips, each 9½" x 42", for catchall body
  1 strip, 9½" x 15", for catchall pocket
From the ribbon, cut:
  4 strips, each 15"
  2 strips, each 8"

Assembling the Catchall

1. On the 9½" x 15" pocket piece, measure up
   7" from one short end and 4" over from each
   side. Make a mark at each point to indicate
   the buttonhole placements. Then make a
   ½"-long buttonhole at each mark.

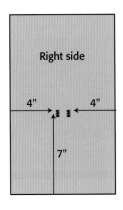

2. Press the pocket rectangle in half, wrong
   sides together and raw edges even, to make a
   9½" x 7½" piece. To make the casing, stitch
   ⅛" from the fold; then stitch ¾" from the
   stitched line. Thread one 8" piece of ribbon
   through the casing and out the nearest buttonhole. Repeat with the opposite side.
   With the ribbon raw edges even with the
   fabric raw edges, baste the ribbon in place.

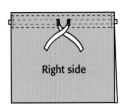

3. Stitch the 9½" x 42" body pieces, right
   sides together, along one short end to make
   one long strip. If you are working with a
   striped fabric, be sure to match the pattern.
   Trim the long piece to 9½" x 58". With raw

edges even and right sides up, lay the folded pocket at one end of the body piece.

Right side

4. Fold the strip in half, right sides together, so the short ends meet. Stitch ¼" from the outer edge, leaving a 4" opening on one side for turning. Be careful not to catch the loose tie ends in the stitching.

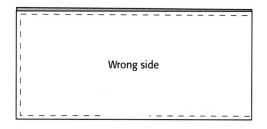

Wrong side

5. Clip the corners on the diagonal, turn the catchall to the right side, and press. Top-stitch ⅛" from the edges.

6. Press one end of each 15" length of ribbon under ½". Position the pressed-under edge on each side of the catchall at the pocket upper edge. Center the remaining 2 pieces on each side of the catchall between the pocket upper edge and the opposite body end. Stitch the ribbon ties in place by using an X-stitch formation for added strength.

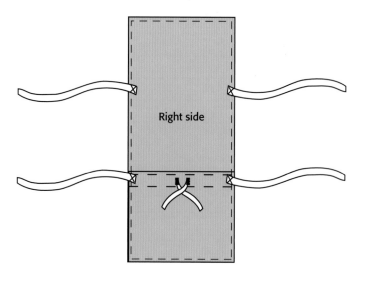

Right side

7. Cut the loose ribbon ends at an angle. Tie each end in a knot. Pull the pocket ties up to slightly gather the upper pocket edge; tie.

8. Lay the catchall over the chair. Tie corresponding 15" ribbon length in a bow.

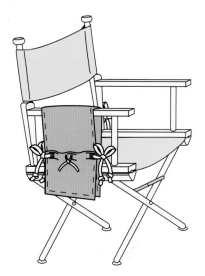

CHAIR COVERS

Remove existing covers from your chairs to determine yardage requirements and patterns. Sew new covers; then add a quick-to-make headrest pillow (page 68). Give a fresh, new appearance to your porch.

HEADREST PILLOW

Finished Pillow Size: 18" x 8"

Materials

42"-wide fabric

¼ yd. muslin for pillow form
¼ yd. fabric of your choice for pillow cover
Polyester fiberfill

Cutting

All measurements include ¼"-wide seam allowances.

From the muslin, cut:

2 strips, each 8" x 18", for pillow form

From the pillow-cover fabric, cut:

1 strip, 8½" x 38", for pillow cover
2 strips, each 2" x 26½", for ties

Assembling the Headrest Pillow

1. Refer to "Throw-Pillow Finishing" on page 17 to stitch the muslin pieces together for the pillow form.

2. To make the pillow cover, turn under a ½" hem on each 8½" end of the pillow-cover strip.

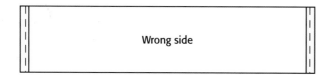

Wrong side

3. Refer to "Ties" on page 18 to make the ties with the 2" x 26½" strips.

4. Center the finished ties on the pillow-cover right side, parallel to and 6" from each 8½" end. Sew the ties in place, stitching to within ½" of the long raw edges.

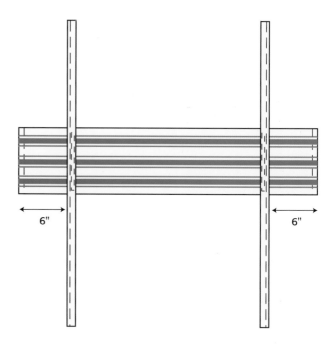

6"   6"

5. With right sides together, fold the pillow-cover ends to the center of the strip. Overlap the ends 1". With the ties out of the seam line, stitch along each side, ¼" from the edge. Turn the cover right side out. Insert the pillow form through the center back opening.

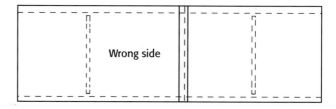

Wrong side

6. Tie the finished pillow to the head of the chair.

COLLAPSIBLE FABRIC BAG

Finished Size: 19" x 13"

Materials

42"-wide fabric

1¼ yds. floral print for bag body

1¼ yds. coordinating striped print for bag body and binding

1¼ yds. solid color for lining

Cutting

All measurements include ¼"-wide seam allowances.

From the floral print, cut:

   3 rectangles, each 13½" x 19½", for bag body

   2 squares, each 13½" x 13½", for bag body

From the coordinating striped-print fabric, cut*:

   4 strips on the lengthwise grain, each 3¼" x 19½", for bag body

   4 strips on the lengthwise grain, each 3¼" x 13½", for bag body

From the solid color fabric, cut:

   3 rectangles, each 9½" x 13½", for lining

   2 squares, each 13½" x 13½", for lining

*Cut the pieces so the pattern will match when the pieces are stitched together (refer to step 2 in "Assembling the Bag" at right).

Assembling the Bag

1. Stitch 2 floral bag body squares and 2 floral bag body rectangles together as shown. Repeat with 2 lining squares and 2 lining rectangles. Press the seam allowances open. Set the remaining body rectangle and lining rectangle aside for the bag bottom. Set the pieced lining strip aside.

19½"	13½"	19½"	13½"

2. Stitch 4 striped bag body strips together as shown. Make 2 pieced strips. Press the seam allowances open. Press under ¼" on one long edge of each pieced strip.

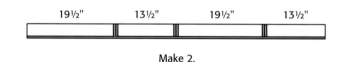

Make 2.

3. With right sides together, stitch a pieced striped strip to the top and bottom edges of the pieced floral strip. Press the seam allowances toward the striped strips. Topstitch the striped strips ⅛" from the seam line.

4. With right sides together and stripes aligned, stitch the short ends together to form a tube. This piece will be the bag sides. Stitch the short ends of the bag lining together to form a tube.

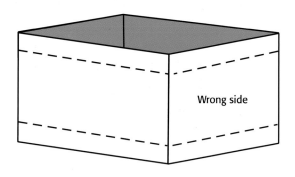

Wrong side

5. Pin the remaining bag body rectangle to the bottom edges of the body side piece, right sides together; stitch. Stitch the remaining lining rectangle to the lining tube in the same manner.

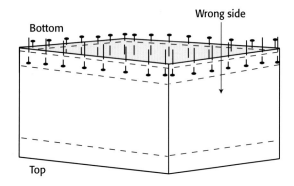

Wrong side

Bottom

Top

6. Pin the lining and body pieces wrong sides together, matching the seam lines and raw edges. Baste in place along the top raw edges.

7. To make the handles, measure in 5" from the side seams and 4" down from the top of the bag on each short end. Draw a rectangle

1½" deep. Stitch along the drawn line, using a short stitch length.

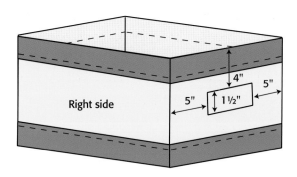

Right side

4" 5"

5" 1½"

8. Cut ¼" inside the rectangle stitching line. Clip the corners diagonally, clipping up to, but not through, the stitching.

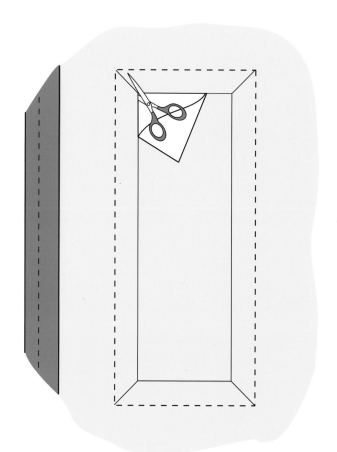

9. From the remaining striped print fabric, make 3 yards of 2½"-wide bias binding (refer to "Finishing the Edges" on page 15). Cut one end of the binding strip at a 45° angle. Press the angled end under ¼". This will be the beginning of the strip. Press the binding strip in half lengthwise, wrong sides together, aligning the raw edges.

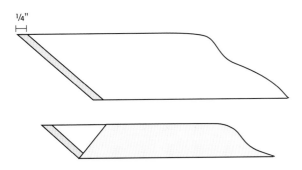

¼"

10. With right sides together and raw edges even, place the pressed under end of the binding strip along the bag upper edge. Begin stitching 2" from the binding end, and end stitching approximately 2" from the beginning of the binding strip, leaving the needle down in the fabric. Trim the end of the binding so it overlaps the beginning by 2". Tuck the cut end of the binding strip inside the diagonal fold. Be sure that the join is smooth on the long folded edge. Pin, then finish sewing the binding to the bag. Fold the binding to the bag lining side and whipstitch the folded edge in place.

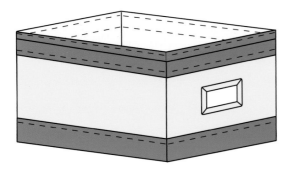

11. Unfold the remaining strip of binding. Cut one end at a 45° angle. Follow step 9 to prepare the binding for finishing the handle opening edges. Repeat step 10 to attach the binding to the handle opening edges, pivoting at each corner. Before turning the binding to the lining side, clip into the corners, clipping up to but not through the stitching. Fold the binding to the bag lining side and whipstitch the folded edge in place, mitering each corner.

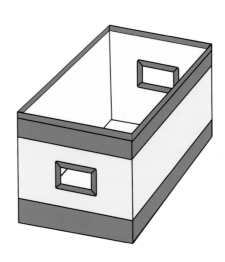

WATERING CAN

Acrylic Paint Palette

DecoArt Americana: #DA184 French Vanilla, #DA 208 Celery Green

Delta Ceramcoat: Metal Primer, #2095 English Yew Green

Plaid FolkArt: #753 Rose Chiffon

Materials

Galvanized watering can
Vinegar
Paintbrushes: #10/0 Liner, #8 and #14 Flat
Matte-finish acrylic spray sealer

Surface Preparation

1. Wash the watering can with a 50 percent vinegar/50 percent water mixture. Rinse with clean water; dry with a clean cloth.
2. Follow the manufacturer's instructions to prime the watering-can outer surface with Metal Primer.

Painting the Design

1. Referring to the photo for placement, paint the midsection and spout with French Vanilla. With English Yew Green, paint a wide stripe through the center of both handles and along the upper portion of the base. Paint the spout head, the outer stripes on the handles, and around the can opening with Celery Green. Paint the remaining stripes on the base and spout with Celery Green, Rose Chiffon, and English Yew Green.
2. Follow the manufacturer's instructions to apply several coats of acrylic spray sealer to the painted surfaces.

PLANTER

Acrylic Paint Palette

Delta Ceramcoat: Metal Primer, #2035 Flesh Tan, #2098 Tomato Spice, #2131 Nightfall Blue

Materials

Galvanized planter
Vinegar
Paintbrushes: #8 and #14 Flat
Matte-finish acrylic spray sealer

Surface Preparation

1. Wash the planter with a 50 percent vinegar/50 percent water mixture. Rinse with clean water; dry with a clean cloth.
2. Follow the manufacturer's instructions to prime the entire outer surface of the planter with Metal Primer.

Painting the Design

1. Referring to the photo for placement, paint the center stripe with Flesh Tan. Paint a stripe on each side of the center stripe with Tomato Spice. Paint the remaining portion of the upper and lower sections with Nightfall Blue. With Flesh Tan, paint the rim.
2. Follow the manufacturer's instructions to apply several coats of acrylic spray sealer to the painted surfaces.

FLOWERPOTS

Acrylic Paint Palette

DecoArt Americana: #DA184 French Vanilla, #DA208 Celery Green

Delta Ceramcoat: #2035 Flesh Tan, #2095 English Yew Green, #2098 Tomato Spice, #2131 Nightfall Blue

Plaid FolkArt: #753 Rose Chiffon

Materials

Several terra-cotta flowerpots in the size of your choice

Matte-finish acrylic spray sealer

Paintbrushes: #10/0 Liner, #8 sealer and #14 Flat

Surface Preparation

1. Check the flowerpots to be sure the outer surfaces are free of any dirt and residue. If necessary, wash with mild detergent and water, rinse in clean water, and let dry thoroughly.
2. Follow the manufacturer's instructions to spray the outer surface of each flowerpot with acrylic spray. Be careful not to spray the inside of the flowerpot if it will be used for plants.

Painting the Designs

1. Referring to the photo for inspiration, use either Tomato Spice, French Vanilla, or Celery Green for a base coat. Paint stripes on the upper portion of each flowerpot as desired with any of the remaining paint colors.
2. Follow the manufacturer's instructions to apply several coats of acrylic spray sealer to the painted surface of each flowerpot.

CABINET

Acrylic Paint Palette

DecoArt Americana: #DA184 French Vanilla, #DA208 Celery Green

Delta Ceramcoat: #2095 English Yew Green

Plaid FolkArt: #753 Rose Chiffon

Materials

Unfinished wood cabinet
Sandpaper
Tack cloth
Paintbrushes: #10/0 Liner, #14 Flat, 2" poly-foam
Wood sealer
Matte-finish varnish

Surface Preparation

1. Lightly sand the surface of the cabinet. Wipe with a tack cloth.
2. Seal with wood sealer. Allow the sealer to dry; then sand the surface again and wipe with a tack cloth.

Painting the Design

1. Apply a base coat of French Vanilla to the entire cabinet.

2. Referring to the photo, paint the trim with English Yew Green. To make the stripes, use a #14 flat brush and Rose Chiffon to paint the thick stripe. Using the liner brush, paint a thin line on one side of the Rose Chiffon stripe with Celery Green and the other side of the Rose Chiffon stripe with English Yew Green.

3. Follow the manufacturer's instructions to apply several coats of varnish to the cabinet to seal the paint; use the polyfoam brush.

FALL PORCH

⊱━◈━◉━◈━⊰

Fall brings the senses alive, with the sights of changing foliage, the sounds of children returning to school, and the occasional aroma of pumpkin pie wafting down the street. Of course, you'll want to keep up with Mother Nature by transforming your porch décor. From the quilt that will warm your toes on chilly evenings to the gift bags that are ideal for filling with bottles of herbed vinegar or wine, each of the projects in this chapter is resplendent with fall colors and motifs that reflect the beauty of the season. Take time to enjoy the ever-changing fall scenery around you, on your porch and beyond.

The Basic Nine-Patch Variation Block

The following instructions explain how to construct the basic block that will be used to make the quilt, tablecloth, and pet pillow-cover projects in this ensemble. The directions for each project will tell the length of the strips to cut and how many Nine-Patch Variation blocks to make.

1. Arrange cream, medium-color, and dark-color print 2"-wide strips into Strip Sets A and B as shown. With right sides together, pin and sew each strip set. Press the seams toward the print fabric. Repeat with beige, medium-color, and dark-color print 2"-wide strips. Cut each strip set into 2"-wide segments. For each block you will need to cut 2 segments from Strip Set A and 1 from Strip Set B. The colors of the segments in each block must be identical.

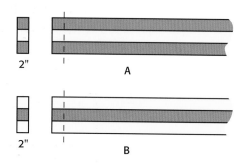

2. Arrange the segments together as shown to make a Nine Patch block. Reverse the direction of each segment so the pressed seams are going in the opposite direction of the previous segment. Sew the segments together. Then press these seams in one direction.

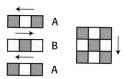

3. Stitch a beige corner triangle to each side of each Nine Patch block with cream background squares. Stitch a cream triangle to each corner of each block with beige background squares. Press the seam allowances toward the triangles.

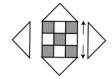

QUILT

Finished Quilt Size: 51" x 70½"
Finished Block Size: 6½" x 6½"

Materials
42"-wide fabric

2 yds. *each* of cream solid and beige solid for
 blocks, inner border, and outer border
7 fat quarters *total* of medium- and dark-color
 prints for blocks and outer border
3½ yds. fabric for backing
Twin-size batting (72" x 90")
⅝ yd. dark print for binding

Cutting

*All measurements include ¼"-wide seam
allowances.*

From *both* the cream solid and beige solid, cut:
 21 strips, each 2" x 21", for blocks and outer
  border
 70 squares, each 4⅛" x 4⅛"; cut in half diagonally to make 140 triangles for block
  corners
 17 strips, each 1¾" x 7", for inner border
 2 squares, each 1¾" x 1¾", for inner border
  corner squares
From *each* of the 7 fat quarters, cut:
 7 strips, each 2" x 21", for blocks and outer
  border
From the backing fabric, cut:
 2 pieces, each 42" x 55"
From the dark print for binding, cut:
 6 strips, each 2½" x 42"

Assembling the Quilt Top

1. Refer to "The Basic Nine-Patch Variation
 Block" on page 82 to use the 2" x 21" cream

solid strips and 2" x 21" strips from the
assorted fat-quarter prints to make 7 of Strip
Set A and 7 of Strip Set B. You will make 1
A strip set and 1 B strip set from each of the
7 fat quarters. Repeat this process with the
2" x 21" beige solid strips and remaining
2" x 21" fat-quarter strips.

2. Cut each Strip Set A into 10 segments.
 Cut each Strip Set B into 5 segments. Set the
 remainder of B strip sets aside for the outer
 border. Stitch the segments together to make
 the Nine Patch blocks. Add the corner triangles to make the Nine-Patch Variation block.
 Make 70 blocks total.

3. Arrange the blocks into 10 horizontal
 rows of 7 blocks each. Alternate the position
 of the blocks with cream corners and the
 blocks with beige corners as shown. Stitch the
 blocks into rows. Stitch the rows together.

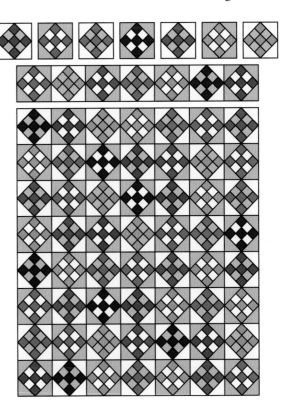

4. To make the inner border side strips, alternately stitch together 5 cream and 5 beige 1¾" x 7" strips as shown. Make 2. To make the inner top border, alternately stitch together 4 beige and 3 cream 1¾" x 7" strips, beginning and ending with a beige strip. Stitch a cream 1¾" x 1¾" square to each end of the strip. Make 1. For the inner bottom border, stitch the remaining 1¾" x 7" strips together, beginning and ending with a cream strip. Stitch a beige 1¾" x 1¾" square to each end of the strip. Make 1.

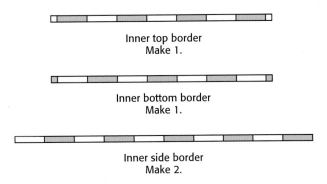

Inner top border
Make 1.

Inner bottom border
Make 1.

Inner side border
Make 2.

5. To make the outer borders, randomly cut a total of 52 segments from the remaining Strip Set B units, each 2" wide. From the remaining cream or beige fabrics, cut 2 squares, each 2" x 2". For the outer side borders, stitch together 15 Strip Set B segments. Make 2.

Outer side border
Make 2.

For the outer top and bottom borders, stitch together 11 Strip Set B segments. Add a cream or beige 2" square to one end of each strip. Make 2.

Outer top/bottom border
Make 2.

6. Refer to "Adding Borders" on page 12 to stitch the inner and outer borders to the quilt top.

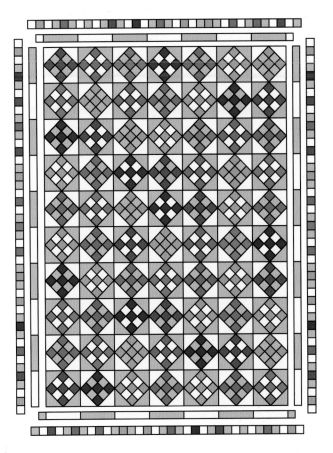

Finishing the Quilt

1. Refer to "Choosing Batting and Backing" on page 13 to stitch the backing pieces together along the long edges to make 1 piece, 55" x 83½". Trim the pieced backing to 55" x 75".

2. Layer the backing, batting, and quilt top; baste the layers together (see "Assembling the Layers" on page 14).

3. Quilt as desired (see "Quilting" on page 14).

4. French bind the quilt edges (see "Finishing the Edges" on page 15).

TABLECLOTH

Finished Tablecloth Size: 40½" x 40½"
Finished Block Size: 6½" x 6½"

Materials

42"-wide fabric

½ yd. *each* of cream solid and cream print for blocks

8 fat quarters *total* or scraps of medium- and dark-color prints for blocks

⅜ yd. dark brown plaid print for inner border

⅞ yd. beige solid for outer border

¼ yd. *each* of 3 assorted brown plaid prints for oak leaves

⅛ yd. or scraps of gold print for acorns

⅛ yd. or scraps of dark brown print for acorn caps

2½ yds. flannel for backing

⅜ yd. light brown print for binding

½ yd. fusible web

Cutting

All measurements include ¼"-wide seam allowances.

From both the cream solid and cream print, cut:
24 strips, each 2" x 10", for blocks
16 squares, each 4⅛" x 4⅛"; cut in half diagonally to make 32 triangles for block corners

From *each* of the 8 fat quarters, cut:
6 strips, each 2" x 10", for blocks

From the dark brown plaid print, cut:
2 strips, each 2" x 26½", for inner side borders
2 strips, each 2" x 29½", for inner top and bottom borders

From the beige solid, cut:
2 strips, each 6" x 29½", for outer side borders
2 strips, each 6" x 40½", for outer top and bottom borders

From the flannel, cut:
2 pieces, each 42" x 45"

From the light brown print, cut:
4 strips, each 2½" x 42", for binding

Assembling the Tablecloth

1. Refer to "The Basic Nine-Patch Variation Block" on page 82 to use the 2" x 10" cream solid strips and 2" x 10" assorted fat-quarter strips to make 8 each of Strip Sets A and B. You will make 1 A and B strip set from *each* of the 8 fat quarters. Repeat this process with the cream-print 2" x 10" strips and the remaining 2" x 10" fat-quarter strips.

2. Cut 2 segments from each Strip Set A and 1 segment from each Strip Set B. Stitch the segments together to make the Nine Patch blocks. Add the corner triangles to each block. Make 16 Nine-Patch Variation blocks total.

3. Arrange the blocks into 4 rows of 4 blocks each. Alternate the position of the blocks with cream corners and the blocks with beige corners as shown. Stitch the blocks into rows. Stitch the rows together.

4. Refer to "Adding Borders" on page 12 to stitch the inner and outer borders to the quilt top.

5. Refer to "Fusible-Web Appliqué" on page 10 to trace the patterns on page 123 onto the paper side of the fusible web. You will need to trace 8 of A and 12 each of B and C. Cut around the motifs. Fuse each motif to the appropriate fabric. Follow the appliqué assembly diagram below to assemble each leaf cluster appliqué. Refer to the photo to fuse a cluster to each corner of the tablecloth. Machine blanket stitch the motifs in place. If you prefer, you may hand appliqué the motifs (see "Hand Appliqué" on pages 11–12).

Finishing the Tablecloth

1. Refer to "Choosing Batting and Backing" on page 13 to stitch the backing pieces together along the long edges to make 1 piece, 45" x 83½". Trim the pieced backing to 45" x 45".
2. Layer the backing and quilt top; baste the layers together (see "Assembling the Layers" on page 14).
3. Quilt as desired (see "Quilting" on page 14).
4. French bind the quilt edges (see "Finishing the Edges" on page 15).

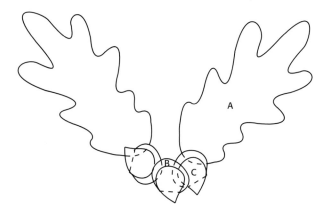

Appliqué assembly diagram

THROW PILLOW

Finished Size: 23½" x 17½"

Materials
42"-wide fabric

⅛ yd. or scraps of 3 assorted plaid prints for oak leaves

⅛ yd. or scraps of gold print for acorns

⅛ yd. or scraps of brown print for acorn caps

¾ yd. beige solid for pillow center rectangle and pillow back

¼ yd. *total* of 4 assorted plaid prints for inner border

¼ yd. *total* of 8 assorted plaid prints for outer border

18" x 24" piece of batting

¼ yd. fusible web

Polyester fiberfill

Cutting

All measurements include ¼"-wide seam allowances.

From the beige solid, cut:

1 rectangle, 12" x 18", for pillow center rectangle

1 rectangle, 18" x 24", for pillow back

From the 4 assorted plaid prints, cut a total of:

2 strips, each 2" x 12", for inner side borders

2 strips, each 2" x 21", for inner top and bottom borders

From the 8 assorted plaid prints, cut a total of:

2 strips, each 2" x 10½", for outer side borders

2 strips, each 2" x 5", for outer side borders

2 strips, each 2" x 14½", for outer top and bottom borders

2 strips, each 2" x 10", for outer top and bottom borders

Assembling the Pillow Top

1. Refer to "Fusible-Web Appliqué" on page 10 to trace the patterns on page 123 onto the paper side of the fusible web. You will need to trace 4 of A and 6 each of B and C. Cut around the motifs. Fuse each motif to the appropriate fabric. Follow the appliqué assembly diagram on page 88 to assemble each leaf cluster appliqué. Refer to the photo to fuse a cluster to opposite corners of the 12" x 18" center rectangle. Machine blanket stitch the motifs in place. If you prefer, you may hand appliqué the motifs (see "Hand Appliqué" on pages 11–12).

2. Refer to "Adding Borders" on page 12 to stitch the inner borders to the pillow center rectangle. To make the outer side borders, stitch the ends of a 2" x 5" strip and a 2" x 10½" strip together to make 1 long strip. Make 2. For the outer top and bottom borders, stitch the ends of a 2" x 10" strip and a 2" x 14½" strip together to make 1 long strip. Make 2. Refer to "Adding Borders" on page 12 to stitch the outer borders to the pillow top.

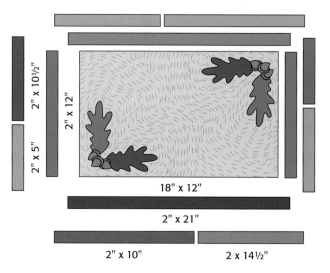

3. Refer to "Throw-Pillow Finishing" on page 17 to complete the pillow.

PET PILLOW

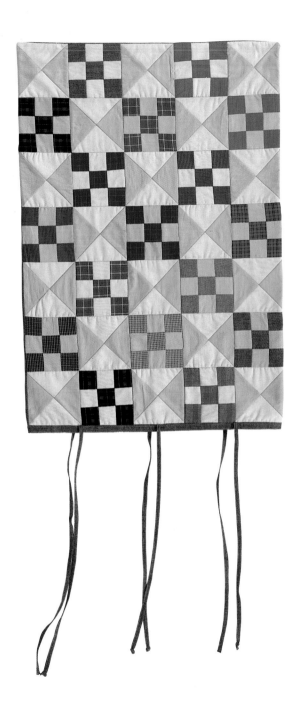

Finished Pillow-Cover Size: 22½" x 31½"
Finished Block Size: 4½" x 4½"

Materials
42"-wide fabric

⅝ yd. *each* of cream solid and beige solid for blocks

9 fat quarters *total* or scraps of medium- and dark-color prints

26" x 35" piece of batting

⅞ yd. muslin for pillow-top backing

⅞ yd. fabric for pillow back

¼ yd. dark print for ties and binding

Standard-size pillow

Cutting

All measurements include ¼"-wide seam allowances.

From the cream solid, cut:

    2 strips, each 2" x 42"; crosscut to make 32 squares, each 2" x 2", for Nine Patch blocks

    9 squares, each 5¾" x 5¾", for Hourglass blocks

From the beige solid, cut:

    2 strips, each 2" x 42"; crosscut to make 36 squares, each 2" x 2", for Nine Patch blocks

    9 squares, each 5¾" x 5¾", for Hourglass blocks

From each of the 9 fat quarters, cut:

    10 squares, each 2" x 2", for Nine Patch blocks

From the muslin, cut:

    1 piece, 26" x 35", for pillow-top backing

From the pillow-back fabric, cut:

    1 piece, 23" x 32"

From the dark print, cut:
  6 strips, each 2" x 18", for ties
  2 strips, each 2½" x 42", for binding

Assembling the Pet Pillow Cover

1. To make the Nine Patch blocks, assemble 4 cream or beige 2" x 2" squares and 5 fat-quarter 2" x 2" squares of the same color into 3 rows of 3 blocks each as shown. Stitch the squares into rows. Stitch the rows together. Make 8 blocks with cream squares and 9 blocks with beige squares (17 blocks total).

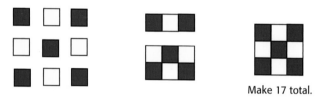

Make 17 total.

2. To make the Hourglass blocks, mark 2 diagonal lines on the wrong side of each cream 5¾" square. Place each cream square on a beige 5¾" square, right sides together. Stitch ¼" from each side of one of the marked lines. Cut each square into quarters, cutting along the unstitched line first. Press each quarter open to make a pieced triangle, pressing the seam toward the beige fabric. Make 36 pieced triangles total. Stitch 2 pieced triangles together as shown to make the Hourglass block. Press the seam allowance in one direction. Make 18 total.

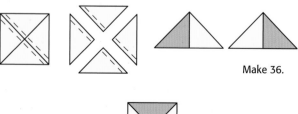

Make 36.

Make 18.

3. Stitch the Nine Patch and Hourglass blocks into 7 horizontal rows of 5 blocks each. Alternate the block position in each row as shown. Press the seam allowances in one direction.

4. Refer to "Pet Pillow-Cover Finishing" on page 17 to finish constructing the pillow cover, quilting the layers together as desired.

5. Insert pillow into cover and tie corresponding ties together into a bow.

GIFT BAGS

Materials

42"-wide fabric

FOR THE LARGE BAG

⅝ yd. fabric for bag body
⅜ yd. contrasting fabric for upper band and tie
Scraps of assorted fabrics for oak leaf, acorn, and acorn cap appliqués
¼ yd. fusible web

FOR THE SMALL BAG

⅜ yd. fabric for bag body
⅜ yd. contrasting fabric for upper band and tie
Scraps of assorted fabrics for oak leaf, acorn, and acorn cap appliqués
¼ yd. fusible web

Cutting

All measurements include ¼"-wide seam allowances.

FOR THE LARGE BAG

From the bag body fabric, cut:
1 piece, 16" x 18"
From the contrasting fabric, cut:
1 piece, 8" x 18", for upper band
1 strip, 2" x 40", for tie

FOR THE SMALL BAG

From the bag body fabric, cut:
1 piece, 9" x 18"
From the contrasting fabric, cut:
1 piece, 5½" x 18", for upper band
1 strip, 2" x 40", for tie

Assembling the Gift Bag

Note: Instructions for both size bags are the same, with changes for the small bag shown in parenthesis.

1. Measure ½" down from the center of one 18"-long edge of the bag body piece. Mark ½" on either side of the center point and make a ½"-long buttonhole on the right side of fabric at each mark.

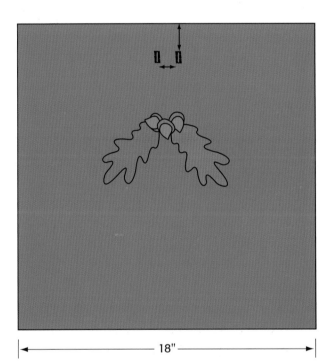

2. Refer to "Fusible-Web Appliqué" on page 10 to trace the patterns on page 123 onto the paper side of the fusible web. You will need to trace 2 of A and 3 each of B and C. Cut around the motifs. Fuse each motif to the appropriate fabric. Follow the appliqué assembly diagram on page 88 to assemble the leaf cluster appliqué. Referring to the photo, center and fuse the cluster to the bag

body 3" to 4" below the buttonholes. Machine blanket stitch the motifs in place. If you prefer, you may hand appliqué the motifs (see "Hand Appliqué" on pages 11–12).

3. Fold the bag body in half, right sides together, matching the 16" (9") edges; stitch the 16" (9") edges together. Press the seam allowance open.

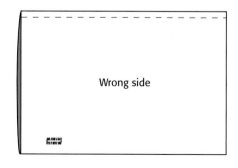

Wrong side

4. Press one long edge of the upper band piece under ¼". Stitch in place, close to the raw edge. Fold the band in half, right sides together, with the short edges matching; stitch the short edges together. Turn the band right side out. Press the seam allowance open.

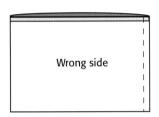

Wrong side

5. With right sides together and raw edges and seams matching, place the upper band inside the bag body piece; stitch. Lay the bag body as shown with the back seam centered and bag bottom raw edges matching; stitch.

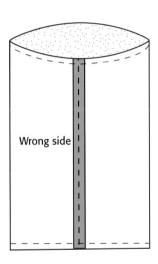

Wrong side

6. Fold the upper band to the wrong side of the bag body so the pressed-under edge is 1½" below the upper edge seam line. Stitch in

place close to the hemmed edge and in the ditch of the bag/band seam line.

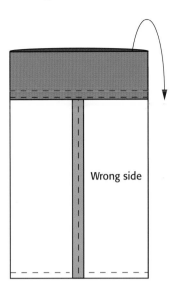

Wrong side

7. To square the bag bottom, open out the bag bottom so the seam line is flat as shown. Mark 1" in from each end of the seam line. Draw a line across this, creating a triangle at each end. Stitch across the line.

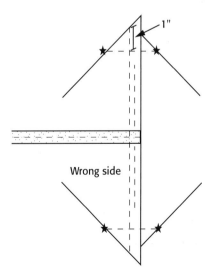

1"

Wrong side

8. Turn the bag right side out. Refer to "Ties" on page 18 to make the tie. Insert one end of the tie through one of the buttonholes and out the opposite buttonhole. Knot the tie ends.

CHAIR PLANTER

Acrylic Paint Palette

DecoArt Americana: #DA157 Black Green, #DA174 Milk Chocolate

Delta Ceramcoat: #2010 Forest Green, #2065 Apple Green, #2063 Spice Tan, #2024 Walnut, #2506 Black

Materials

Old wood chair with open seat
Sandpaper
Tack cloth
Wood sealer
Paintbrushes: #8 and #14 Flat
Matte-finish varnish
1 yd. green burlap
Upholstery tacks
Dried sphagnum moss
Soil and assorted plants or assorted dried florals, fruits, and vegetables

Surface Preparation

1. Sand the surfaces that will be painted. Wipe with a tack cloth.
2. Seal with wood sealer. Let dry; then lightly sand again. Wipe with a tack cloth.

Painting the Design

1. Apply a base coat of Black to the appropriate areas. Refer to the photograph for suggestions.
2. Transfer the patterns on page 123 to the chair where desired.

3. Paint the leaves Forest Green. Shade the leaves with Black Green and highlight with Apple Green. Paint the acorns with Spice Tan. Shade the acorns with Milk Chocolate. Paint the acorn caps with Milk Chocolate. Shade the acorn caps with Walnut and highlight with Spice Tan.
4. Follow the manufacturer's instructions to apply 2 coats of varnish to the painted surfaces.
5. Fold the burlap so it is doubled. Drape the burlap across the seat opening, letting it drop down into the opening about 6". Tack the burlap to the chair seat with the upholstery tacks. Trim away any excess burlap.

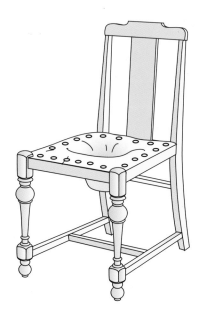

6. Lay sphagnum moss on the bottom and sides of the opening. Fill the opening with soil and assorted plants or dried florals, fruits, and vegetables.
7. Position the chair in an area where it will not get wet and will be away from direct sunlight.

LAMP SHADE

Acrylic Paint Palette

DecoArt Americana: #DA157 Black Green, #DA174 Milk Chocolate

Delta Ceramcoat: #2010 Forest Green, #2065 Apple Green, #2063 Spice Tan, #2024 Walnut, #2506 Black

Materials

Purchased lamp shade
Paintbrushes: #8 and #14 Flat
Matte-finish acrylic spray sealer

Painting the Design

1. Apply a base coat of Black to the lamp shade.
2. Transfer the patterns on page 123 to the lamp shade where desired.
3. Paint the leaves Forest Green. Shade the leaves with Black Green and highlight with Apple Green. Paint the acorns with Spice Tan. Shade the acorns with Milk Chocolate. Paint the acorn caps with Milk Chocolate. Shade the acorn caps with Walnut and highlight with Spice Tan.
4. Follow the manufacturer's instructions to apply several coats of sealer to the lamp shade.

WINTER PORCH

Even if you live in an area plagued with mounds of the white fluffy stuff, there's no reason to let Old Man Winter chase you indoors. In fact, this cheery winter porch ensemble is sure to be so inviting you'll want to spend every available moment relaxing in the cozy atmosphere the projects create. And for those of you who have escaped to regions where snow is seldom-if-ever seen, this chapter offers you a mound of warm and welcome flakes that will melt your heart.

The Basic Snowflake Block

The following instructions explain how to construct the basic block that will be used to make the stitched projects in this ensemble. The directions for each project tell how many Snowflake blocks to make.

To make each block, you will need a small amount of several off-white, cream, and ecru prints and solids, as well as 4 dark blue prints and 1 medium blue print. Each specific project tells you exactly how much fabric you will need.

Assembling the Block

1. Stitch medium blue 2⅛" half-square triangles to the top and one side of a dark blue 1¾" square as shown. Press the seam allowances toward the triangles. Make 8.

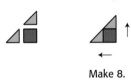

Make 8.

2. Stitch an off-white, cream, or ecru 3⅜" half-square triangle to the pieced unit from step 1. Press the seam allowance toward the light triangle.

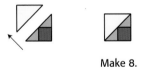

Make 8.

3. To make each quarter of the block, stitch an off-white, cream, or ecru 3" square to 2 of the pieced units as shown. Press the seam allowance toward the light squares. Stitch the units together as shown. Press the seam allowance in one direction. Make 4.

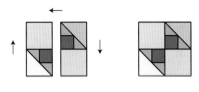

Make 4.

4. Arrange the 4 pieced units together into 2 rows of 2 units each, rotating the units as shown. Stitch the units into rows. Press the seam allowances in opposite directions. Stitch the rows together, being careful to match the center points. Stitch; then press the seam allowances in one direction to make 1 Snowflake block.

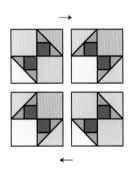

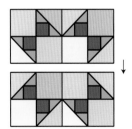

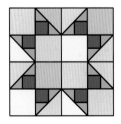

QUILT

Finished Quilt Size: 55" x 75"
Finished Block Size: 10" x 10"

Materials

42"-wide fabric

½ yd. *each* of 10 assorted off-white, cream, and ecru solids and prints for Snowflake blocks, Four Patch blocks, and border

1⅛ yds. medium blue print for Snowflake blocks and binding

1 fat quarter *each* of 4 assorted dark blue prints for Snowflake blocks

3¾ yds. fabric for backing

59" x 79" piece of batting

Cutting

All measurements include ¼"-wide seam allowances.

From the off-white, cream, and ecru solids and prints, cut a total of:

68 squares, each 5½" x 5½", for Four Patch blocks

72 squares, each 3⅜" x 3⅜"; cut in half diagonally to make 144 half-square triangles for Snowflake blocks

244 squares, each 3" x 3", for Snowflake blocks and border

From the medium blue print, cut:

144 squares, each 2⅛" x 2⅛"; cut in half diagonally to make 288 half-square triangles for Snowflake blocks

7 strips, each 2½" x 42", for binding

From the dark blue prints, cut a total of:

144 squares, each 1¾" x 1¾", for Snowflake blocks

From the backing fabric, cut:

2 pieces, each 42" x 59"

Assembling the Quilt Top

1. Refer to "The Basic Snowflake Block" on page 103 to use the off-white, cream, and ecru 3" squares and half-square triangles, the medium blue half-square triangles, and the assorted dark blue-print 1¾" squares to make 18 Snowflake blocks.

2. Randomly arrange 4 off-white, cream, or ecru 5½" squares together as shown to make a Four Patch block. Press the seams in the direction shown. Make 17.

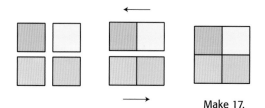

Make 17.

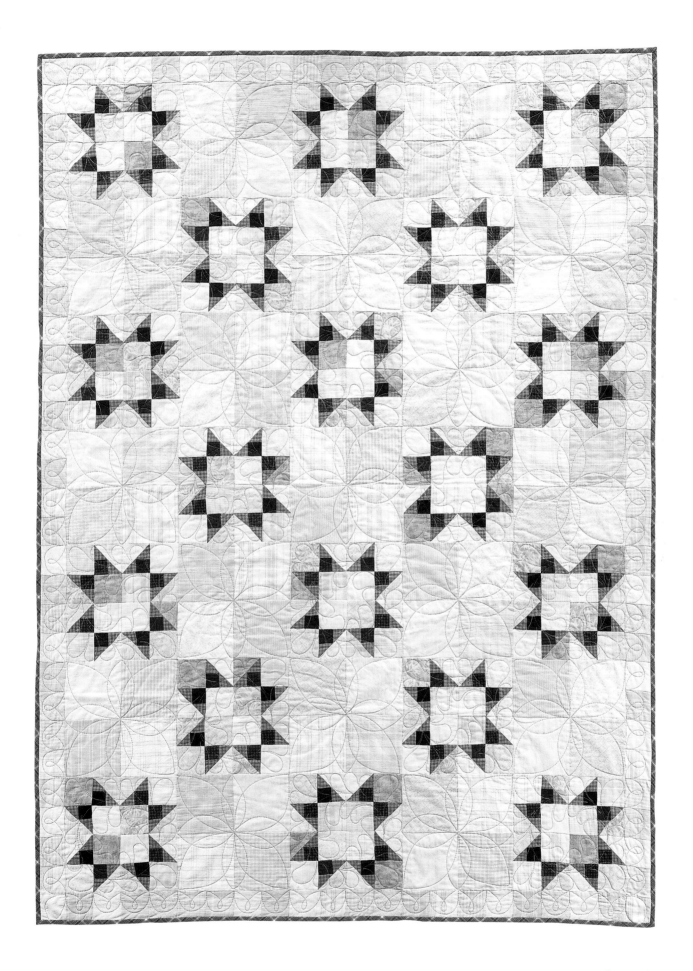

3. Arrange the Snowflake and Four Patch blocks into 7 horizontal rows of 5 blocks each. Alternate the blocks in each row as shown. Stitch the blocks into rows. Press the seam allowances in the opposite directions from row to row. Stitch the rows together. Press the seam allowances in one direction.

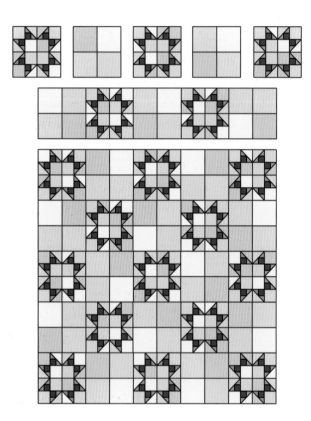

4. To make the outer side borders, randomly stitch 28 off-white, cream, or ecru 3" squares together end to end to make one long strip. Measure the strip to be sure it is 70½" long. Press the seam allowances in one direction. Make 2. For the outer top and bottom borders, randomly stitch 22 off-white, cream, or ecru 3" squares together end to end to make one long strip. Measure the strip to be sure it is 55½" long. Press the seam allowances in one direction. Make 2.

5. Refer to "Adding Borders" on page 12 to stitch the borders to the quilt top.

Finishing the Quilt

1. Refer to "Choosing Batting and Backing" on page 13 to stitch the backing pieces together along the long edges to make 1 piece, 59" x 83½".

2. Layer the backing, batting, and quilt top; baste the layers together (see "Assembling the Layers" on page 14).

3. Quilt as desired (see "Quilting" on page 14).

4. French bind the quilt edges (see "Finishing the Edges" on page 15).

WALL HANGING

Finished Wall Hanging Size: 30" x 30"
Finished Block Size: 10" x 10"

Materials
42"-wide fabric

1 fat quarter *each* of 6 assorted off-white, cream, and ecru solids and prints for blocks

¼ yd. *each* of 1 medium blue and 1 dark blue print for blocks

¼ yd. tan print for inner border

⅝ yd. beige print for outer border

½ yd. medium blue print for outer border letters

1 yd. backing fabric

34" x 34" square of batting

⅜ yd. tan print for binding

½ yd. fusible web

Cutting

All measurements include ¼"-wide seam allowances.

From the off-white, cream, and ecru solids and prints, cut a *total* of:
32 squares, each 3" x 3", for blocks
16 squares, each 3⅜" x 3⅜"; cut in half diagonally to make 32 half-square triangles for blocks

From the medium blue print, cut:
32 squares, each 2⅛" x 2⅛"; cut in half diagonally to make 64 half-square triangles for blocks

From the dark blue print, cut:
32 squares, each 1¾" x 1¾", for blocks

From the tan print for inner border, cut:
2 strips, each 1½" x 20½", for sides
2 strips, each 1½" x 22½", for the top and bottom

From the beige print, cut:
2 strips, each 4½" x 22½", for outer side borders
2 strips, each 4½" x 30½", for outer top and bottom borders

From the tan print for binding, cut:
3 strips, each 2½" x 42"

From the backing fabric, cut:
1 piece, 34" x 34"

Assembling the Wall Hanging Top

1. Refer to "The Basic Snowflake Block" on page 103 to use the off-white, cream, and ecru 3" squares and half-square triangles, the medium blue half-square triangles, and the assorted dark blue 1¾" squares to make 4 Snowflake blocks.

2. Arrange the blocks into 2 horizontal rows of 2 blocks each. Stitch the blocks together into rows. Press the seams in opposite directions. Stitch the rows together. Press the seam in one direction.

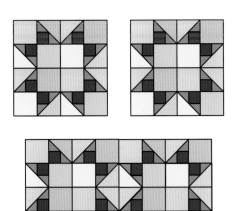

3. Refer to "Adding Borders" on page 12 to stitch the inner and outer borders to the quilt top.

4. Refer to "Fusible-Web Appliqué" on page 10 to trace the patterns on page 125 onto the paper side of the fusible web. You will need to trace enough individual letters to spell out the lyrics "The weather outside is frightful but the fire is so delightful." Cut around the letters. Fuse the letters to the medium blue print. Refer to the appliqué placement diagram below to fuse the letters to the outer border, leaving an equal amount of spacing between each letter and word. Machine blanket stitch the letters in place. If you prefer, you may hand appliqué the motifs (see "Hand Appliqué" on pages 11–12).

Appliqué placement diagram

Finishing the Wall Hanging

1. Layer the backing, batting, and quilt top; baste the layers together (see "Assembling the Layers" on page 14).
2. Quilt as desired (see "Quilting" on page 14).
3. French bind the quilt edges (see "Finishing the Edges" on page 15).

CHENILLE RUG

Chenille is made up of seven to eight layers of unwashed fabric that are quilted together at a 45° angle to the straight of grain. Once the layers are quilted, all but the bottom two base layers are slashed through the channels that were created when the fabric was quilted. The piece is then washed and dried, and the combination of shrinking and fraying makes chenille. Quilting cotton, cotton flannel, and rayon are all good candidates for this technique. Experiment with fabric colors and layering order before starting a project. Make 5"-square samples of stacked, stitched, and cut fabrics. Be sure to wash and dry each sample so you can preview the results before making a final project.

Finished Rug Size: Approximately 26" x 38"

Materials
42"-wide fabric

⅞ yd. *each* of 7 or 8 cotton or rayon fabrics (2 fabrics are for the base layers)
90/14 sewing-machine needle
¼ yd. fabric for binding

Cutting

All measurements include ¼"-wide seam allowances.

From the 7 or 8 cotton or rayon fabrics, cut from *each*:
   1 rectangle, 30" x 42"
From the fabric for binding, cut:
   2 strips, each 2½" x 42"

Constructing the Rug

1. Layer 1 base fabric piece right side down. Place the remaining base fabric over the first, right side up. Layer the remaining fabric rectangles over the base fabrics, right side up, in the order determined by the sample block. Press the fabrics after each addition.

2. Pin the layers together. Space the pins about 6" apart, keeping the fabric edges even.

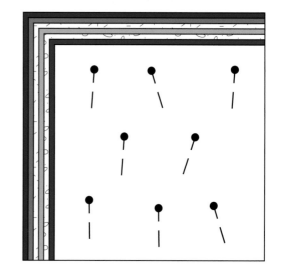

3. Draw a line at a 45° angle to the straight of grain that goes from one corner to the opposite corner. Mark several more lines on each side of the first line as shown, leaving ½" between lines. Fill in the remainder of the rectangle with lines that run perpendicular to the first set of lines but do not intersect them.

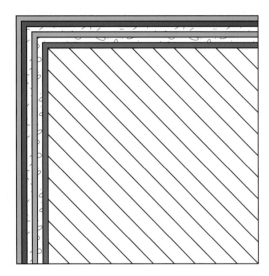

4. Using a size 90/14 needle, stitch along the drawn lines. You may want to lengthen the stitches to feed the fabric through more easily. Reverse the stitching direction for each line.

5. Cut between the stitching lines, cutting all but the two base layers. There are special tools available that will make cutting easier, but a pair of sharp scissors will work.

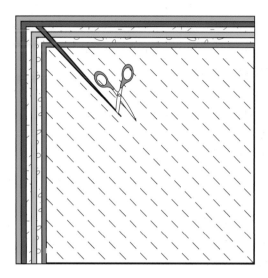

6. Machine baste around the outside edges of the rug. Place the rug in the washing machine by itself. Set the machine for a short cycle, regular or delicate, with a warm wash and cold rinse. Dry the piece by itself in the dryer at a medium setting.

7. Square the rug to size after washing and drying.

8. Bind the rug edges with French binding (see "Finishing the Edges" on page 15).

CHECKERBOARD THROW PILLOW

Finished Pillow Size: 16½" x 16½"

Materials

42"-wide fabric

¼ yd. medium blue print
⅛ yd. *each* or scraps of 2 dark blue prints
¼ yd. blue check print for border
⅝ yd. fabric for pillow back
Polyester fiberfill

Cutting

All measurements include ¼"-wide seam allowances.

From the medium blue print, cut:
   2 strips, each 2" x 42"; crosscut to make 40 squares, each 2" x 2"

From the dark blue prints, cut a *total of*:
   41 squares, each 2" x 2"

From the blue check print, cut:
   2 strips, each 2" x 14", for side borders
   2 strips, each 2" x 17", for top and bottom borders

From the pillow-back fabric, cut:
   1 square, 17" x 17"

Assembling the Pillow

1. Arrange the medium blue and dark blue 2" squares in 9 horizontal rows of 9 squares each. Alternate the block position in each row as shown. Stitch the squares into rows. Press the seams in one direction, alternating the direction for each row. Stitch the rows together.

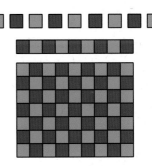

2. Refer to "Adding Borders" on page 12 to stitch the borders to the pillow top.
3. Refer to "Throw-Pillow Finishing" on page 17 to complete the pillow.

SNOWFLAKE THROW PILLOW

QUICK TO STITCH

Finished Pillow Size: 16" x 16"
Finished Block Size: 10" x 10"

Materials

42"-wide fabric

¼ yd. *total* of assorted off-white, cream, and ecru solids and prints for block

⅛ yd. or scraps of medium blue print for block

⅛ yd. *total* or scraps of assorted dark blue prints for block

⅜ yd. cream print for border

⅝ yd. fabric for pillow back

Polyester fiberfill

Cutting

All measurements include ¼"-wide seam allowances.

From the assorted off-white, cream, and ecru solids and prints, cut a *total of:*

8 squares, each 3" x 3", for block

4 squares, each 3⅜" x 3⅜"; crosscut to make 8 half-square triangles for block

From the medium blue print, cut:

8 squares, each 2⅛" x 2⅛"; crosscut to make 16 half-square triangles for block

From the assorted dark blue prints, cut a *total of:*

8 squares, each 1¾" x 1¾", for block

From the cream print, cut:

2 strips, each 3½" x 10½", for side borders

2 strips, each 3½" x 16½", for top and bottom borders

From the pillow-back fabric, cut:

1 square, 16½" x 16½"

Assembling the Pillow

1. Refer to "The Basic Snowflake Block" on page 103 to use the off-white, cream, and ecru 3" squares and half-square triangles, the medium blue half-square triangles, and the assorted dark blue 1¾" squares to make 1 Snowflake block.

2. Refer to "Adding Borders" on page 12 to stitch the borders to the pillow top.

3. Refer to "Throw-Pillow Finishing" on page 17 to complete the pillow.

WINDOW TABLE

Garage sales and antique stores are great places to find old windows and used table legs. Screw a matching set of legs to a window to create a unique table for your porch.

SISAL RUG

Acrylic Paint Palette

Delta Ceramcoat: #2131 Nightfall Blue, #2492 Oyster White

Plaid FolkArt: #607 Settlers Blue

Materials

Purchased sisal rug
Stencil brush
Template plastic
Roller brush

Painting the Design

1. Measure the rug length and width. Then determine the width of the squares for the checkerboard pattern. For example, if the length and width measurements are divisible by 2", then your squares can be 2" wide. Mark the width of the outer and inner borders using these measurements.

2. Paint the checkerboard pattern on the outer and inner border, alternating Settlers Blue and Nightfall Blue. Use the stencil brush to work the paint into the fabric.

3. Transfer the pattern on page 124 to the template plastic. Cut inside the pattern lines to create the stencil.

4. Position the stencil on the rug as desired and use the roller brush to paint the snowflake design with Oyster White.

CHAIRS

Perk up antique lawn chairs by stenciling the Snowflake pattern on page 124 on the back of the chairs. Delta Ceramcoat acrylic paint in Oyster White (#2492) is just the right color to set the mood for winter.

PET PILLOW

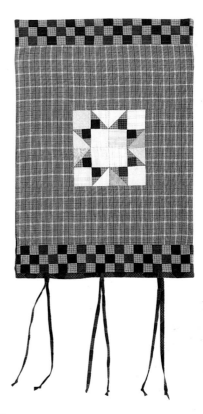

Finished Pillow-Cover Size: 23¾" x 32½"
Finished Block Size: 10" x 10"

Materials
42"-wide fabric

¼ yd. *total* of assorted off-white, cream, and ecru solids and prints for block

⅜ yd. medium blue print for block and top and bottom borders

⅝ yd. dark blue print for block, top and bottom borders, binding, and ties

⅞ yd. medium blue plaid for pillow center panel

29" x 37" piece of batting

1 yd. muslin for pillow-top backing

1 yd. fabric for pillow back

Standard-size pillow

Cutting

All measurements include ¼"-wide seam allowances.

From the assorted off-white, cream, and ecru solids and prints, cut:

    8 squares, each 3" x 3", for block

    4 squares, each 3⅜" x 3⅜"; cut in half diagonally to make 8 half-square triangles for block

From the medium blue print, cut:

    8 squares, each 2⅛" x 2⅛"; cut in half diagonally to make 16 half-square triangles for block

    3 strips, each 1¾" x 42", for top and bottom borders

From the dark blue print, cut:

8 squares, each 1¾" x 1¾", for block

3 strips, each 1¾" x 42", for top and bottom borders

6 strips, each 2" x 18", for ties

2 strips, each 2½" x 42", for binding

From the medium blue plaid, cut:

1 rectangle, 24¼" x 25½"

From the muslin, cut:

1 rectangle, 29" x 37", for pillow-top backing

From the backing fabric, cut:

1 rectangle, 24¼" x 33"

Assembling the Pet Pillow

1. Refer to "The Basic Snowflake Block" on page 103 to use the off-white, cream, and ecru 3" squares and half-square triangles, the medium blue half-square triangles, and the assorted dark blue 1¾" squares to make 1 Snowflake block.

2. Press the edges of the block under ¼" on all sides. Center the block on the pillow center rectangle and stitch close to the block outer edges.

3. To make the upper and lower borders, arrange the medium blue print and dark blue print 1¾" x 42" strips into Strip Sets A and B as shown. With right sides together, pin and sew each strip set. Press the seams in one direction. From Strip Set A, cut 20 segments, each 1¾" wide. From Strip Set B, cut 18 segments, each 1¾" wide.

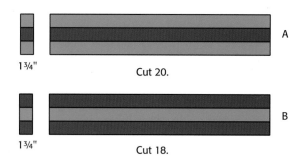

1¾"   Cut 20.   A

1¾"   Cut 18.   B

4. Alternately stitch 10 Strip Set A segments and 9 Strip Set B segments together as shown, beginning and ending with a Strip Set A segment. Be sure border measures 24¼". Make 2.

Make 2.

5. Stitch the borders to the top and bottom of the pillow center panel.

6. Refer to "Pet Pillow-Cover Finishing" on page 17 to complete the pillow cover.

7. Insert the pillow into cover and tie corresponding ties together into a bow.

ENAMELWARE

Acrylic Paint Palette

DecoArt Americana: #DA1 Titanium White

Delta Ceramcoat: Metal Primer, #2506 Black

Plaid FolkArt: #609 Thunder Blue

Materials

Enamelware mugs
Galvanized bucket
Vinegar
Paintbrushes: #2 Round, #14 Flat
Natural sea sponge
Matte-finish acrylic spray sealer

Surface Preparation

1. Wash the mugs with soap and water. Dry thoroughly.
2. Wash the bucket with a 50 percent vinegar/50 percent water mixture. Rinse with clean water; dry with a clean cloth. Follow the manufacturer's instructions to prime the outer surface with Metal Primer.

Painting the Design

1. If the mugs are not already white, sponge the entire outer surfaces with Titanium White. Sponge the bucket lower half with Titanium White and the upper half with Thunder Blue.
2. Using the patterns on page 125, transfer the desired words to the mugs and bucket. Paint the letters with Black. Follow the manufacturer's instructions to apply several coats of acrylic spray to the painted surfaces.

Note: These mugs and bucket make great planters. Fill them with soil and herbs and watch your plants grow.

PATTERNS

Spring Porch

Bee

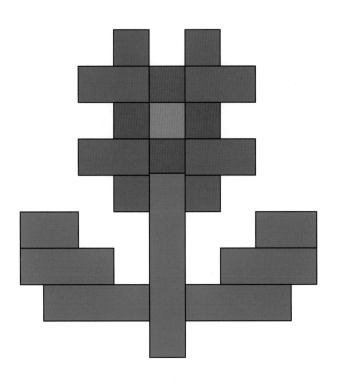

Flower

Fall Porch

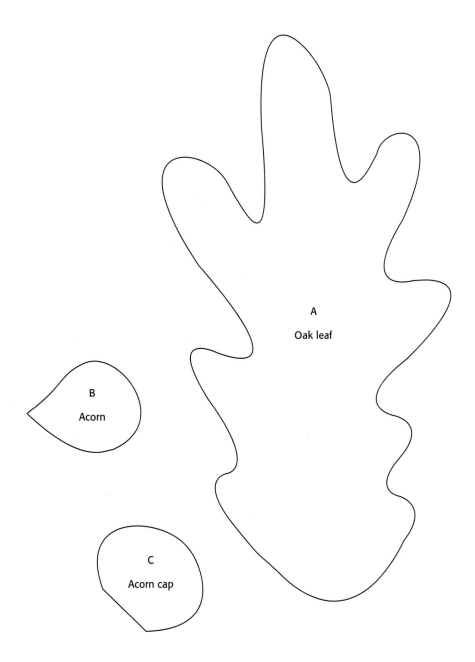

A

Oak leaf

B

Acorn

C

Acorn cap

Snowflake

RESOURCES

Acrylic Paint

Refer to these paint suppliers for answers to specific questions or problems.

Americana
DecoArt
PO Box 386
Stanford, KY 40484
Phone: (800) 477-8478
Fax: (606) 365-9739
www.decoart.com

Ceramcoat
Delta Technical Coatings, Inc.
2550 Pellissier Place
Whittier, CA 90601
Phone: (800) 423-4135
Fax: (562) 695-5157

FolkArt
Plaid Enterprises
3225 Westech Drive
Norcross, GA 30091-0600
Phone: (800) 842-4197
Fax: (678) 291-8384
www.plaidonline.com

Batting

Warm & Natural needlepunch cotton batting
The Warm Company
954 E. Union St.
Seattle, WA 98122
Phone: (800) 234-WARM or (206) 320-9276
Fax: (206) 320-0974
www.warmcompany.com

Fusible Web

HeatnBond Lite
Therm O Web
770 Glenn Ave.
Wheeling, IL 60090
Phone: (800) 323-0799
Fax: (847) 520-0025
www.thermoweb.com

Galvanized Tin

Decorator & Craft Corporation
428 S. Zelta
Wichita, KS 67207
Phone: (800) 835-3013

ABOUT THE AUTHOR

Leslie Beck's American Folk Art designs are widely recognized throughout the country. Her latest focus combines Folk Art and Country with a sophisticated, modern use of color reflected in today's casual American lifestyle. The versatility and timeliness of her art is easily adapted to many decorating projects and products. Leslie is the founding owner of Fiber Mosaics, Inc. The company name reflects her love and talent for combining colors, shapes, and textures.

Leslie welcomes the ever growing and changing future. Her inspiration comes from combining the fibers of life and textures of nature into a mosaic of new ideas

NEW AND BESTSELLING TITLES FROM

America's Best-Loved Craft & Hobby Books™

America's Best-Loved Quilt Books®

QUILTING
From That Patchwork Place, an imprint of Martingale & Company

Appliqué
Artful Appliqué
Colonial Appliqué
Red and Green: An Appliqué Tradition
Rose Sampler Supreme
Your Family Heritage: Projects in
　Appliqué

Baby Quilts
Appliqué for Baby
The Quilted Nursery
Quilts for Baby: Easy as ABC
More Quilts for Baby: Easy as ABC
Even More Quilts for Baby: Easy as ABC

Holiday Quilts
Easy and Fun Christmas Quilts
Favorite Christmas Quilts from That
　Patchwork Place
Paper Piece a Merry Christmas
A Snowman's Family Album Quilt
Welcome to the North Pole

Learning to Quilt
Basic Quiltmaking Techniques for:
　Borders and Bindings
　Curved Piecing
　Divided Circles
　Eight-Pointed Stars
　Hand Appliqué
　Machine Appliqué
　Strip Piecing
The Joy of Quilting
The Quilter's Handbook
Your First Quilt Book (or it should be!)

Paper Piecing
50 Fabulous Paper-Pieced Stars
A Quilter's Ark
Easy Machine Paper Piecing
Needles and Notions
Paper-Pieced Curves
Show Me How to Paper Piece

Rotary Cutting
101 Fabulous Rotary-Cut Quilts
365 Quilt Blocks a Year Perpetual
　Calendar
Fat Quarter Quilts
Lap Quilting Lives!
Quick Watercolor Quilts
Quilts from Aunt Amy
Spectacular Scraps
Time-Crunch Quilts

Small & Miniature Quilts
Bunnies By The Bay Meets Little Quilts
Celebrate! with Little Quilts
Easy Paper-Pieced Miniatures
Little Quilts All Through the House

CRAFTS
From Martingale & Company

300 Papermaking Recipes
The Art of Handmade Paper and
　Collage
The Art of Stenciling
Creepy Crafty Halloween
Gorgeous Paper Gifts
Grow Your Own Paper
Stamp with Style
Wedding Ribbonry

KNITTING
From Martingale & Company

Comforts of Home
Fair Isle Sweaters Simplified
Knit It Your Way
Simply Beautiful Sweaters
Two Sticks and a String
The Ultimate Knitter's Guide
Welcome Home: Kaffe Fassett

COLLECTOR'S COMPASS™
From Martingale & Company

20th Century Glass
'50s Decor
Barbie® Doll
Jewelry

Coming to *Collector's Compass* Spring 2001:

20th Century Dinnerware
American Coins
Movie Star Collectibles
'60s Decor

Our books are available at bookstores and your favorite craft, fabric, yarn, and antiques retailers. If you don't see the title you're looking for, visit us at **www.martingale-pub.com** or contact us at:

1-800-426-3126
International: 1-425-483-3313
Fax: 1-425-486-7596
E-mail: info@martingale-pub.com

For more information and a full list of our titles, visit our Web site or call for a free catalog.